DECORATING
for DINING &
ENTERTAINING

128 Projects & Ideas

The Home Decorating Institute®

Library of Congress Cataloging-in-Publication Data Decorating for dining & entertaining / The Home Decorating Institute.
p. cm. — (Arts & crafts for home decorating) Includes index. ISBN 0-86573-369-4 ISBN 0-86573-370-8 (pbk.)   1. Handicraft.
2. Table setting and decoration. 3. Dining rooms. 4. Household linens. 5. Entertaining. I. Home Decorating Institute (Minnetonka,
Minn.) II. Title: Decorating for dining and entertaining. III. Series.   TT157.D387 1994 642'.8—dc20   94-32785

CONTENTS

Special Occasion Dining

Table Linens

Table Accessories

Decorating the Dining Room

DECORATING FOR DINING & ENTERTAINING

A traditional feast in the dining room and a candlelit terrace party both conjure up beautiful images.

Even a backyard barbecue can be a memorable event when put together with flair. In addition to good food and conversation, delightful surroundings and a creative table setting make an occasion special.

The dining room can be a wonderful place for family and friends to gather, allowing the daily pace to slow down for a while. Although most dining rooms are formal in style, feel free to break with tradition and decorate yours to reflect your personality. Even if your home does not have a dining room, you can create a special place for dining by setting a table in a corner of the living room, next to the kitchen, or even on an enclosed porch.

Plan the table setting so it reflects your style and sets the mood. A beautiful blend of lace and linen, china and crystal, sets the tone for a formal sit-down dinner. On the other hand, a bright Mexican blanket, used as a tablecloth and combined with terra-cotta and earthenware, can signal a carefree fiesta.

THE DINING ROOM

The dining room is no longer reserved just for formal occasions. For the maximum use of this room, it may be dressed up or down, making it appropriate for either formal or casual entertaining.

Even a dining room with elegant traditional furniture, window treatments, and light fixtures can seem less formal if the table appointments and room accessories are changed. Start by choosing ceramic candle holders instead of brass candlebra, for example, and use cotton placemats instead of a tapestry tablecloth. The dining room shown opposite has a formal look, featuring fine fabrics and luxurious accessories. The same room takes on a more casual look on pages 8 and 9.

ELEGANTLY FORMAL

Rich, refined materials add a feeling of elegance to a room. Tapestries and damasks, used for luxurious tablecloths, are combined with accessories in gold leaf, silver, and brass. Fresh flowers are often preferred for the centerpiece, because they are associated with abundance.

Cherry and mahogany woods are often used in elegant traditional dining rooms, but contemporary rooms can look equally elegant with the use of sleek lacquered finishes. If the dining-room furniture is not formal, dress up the room for a special occasion by using cherry, mahogany, or lacquered serving trays and accessories.

Throughout the dining room, a few small room furnishings can echo the formality of the table appointments. A pair of traditional table lamps can be symmetrically placed on the buffet. A half-round table can be draped with a fine tablecloth trimmed in rich bullion fringe.

Several items shown here can be made following the instructions in this book:

1. *Basic table linens (page 37).*
2. *Bishop's-hat napkin fold (page 40).*
3. *Tapestry table linens (page 49).*
4. *Bullion fringe table linens (page 52).*
5. *Tray doily (page 64).*
6. *Candlestick floral arrangements (page 72).*
7. *Gold-leaf accessories (page 91).*
8. *Chargers (page 94).*
9. *Place cards (page 102).*
10. *Bias swags (page 114).*

(Continued)

THE DINING ROOM
(CONTINUED)

LESS FORMAL

Set the tone for carefree dining with colorful tablecoverings, earthenware serving pieces, and accessories in rustic materials. Feel free to abandon the traditional rules for table settings, such as the rigid placement of silverware and glassware; this change will instantly signal a more relaxed atmosphere.

Experiment with other carefree ideas that break the rules, perhaps using the traditional wall sconces as containers for silk ivy or using a Turkish rug as a runner on the side table. The strong use of a theme, such as Southwestern, can help establish the casual mood.

When using the formal dining room for casual entertaining, downplay the formality of the room by minimizing the elegant features and introducing accessories that lend a more casual style. Remove elegant accent pieces, such as brass candlesticks, replacing them with pieces in ceramic, wood, or iron. If the dining-room furniture is too formal, minimize the look by covering the table with a casual cloth. And consider replacing formal pictures and mirrors with abstract art.

Several items shown here can be made following the instructions in this book:

1. *Basic table linens (page 37).*
2. *Hexagonal placemats (page 56).*
3. *Fresh fruit centerpiece (page 78).*
4. *Votive candles with glass stones (page 84).*
5. *Antiqued gold-leaf accessories (page 91).*
6. *Napkin rings (page 98).*
7. *Triangle-point valances (page 118).*

OTHER DINING AREAS

Dining, of course, is not restricted to the dining room. It often extends into other areas of the house. Even if you are fortunate enough to have a separate dining room, it may not always be large enough to accommodate the number of guests. And sometimes you may prefer to entertain outside the dining room, simply for variety.

For some occasions, you may want to serve an entire meal in another room. Or you may prefer to serve appetizers in one location and the main course in another, or to change locations for the dessert course. By becoming open to new possibilities, you can take advantage of a cheerful fireplace, a breezy porch, or a special view, depending on the season or the occasion.

For large parties, the buffet table may be set up in the dining room, with tables for seating the guests placed in other rooms of the house. It is not necessary to seat all the guests in the same room. In fact, it is usually more interesting to set a few small tables in different rooms, creating small conversation groups.

THE LIVING ROOM

The living room is often used for entertaining. You may choose to serve appetizers to your dinner guests in the living room while dining-room preparations are being completed for the entrée. Or, for a change of pace, guests may retire to the living room after the main course of a formal dinner, where dessert and coffee are served in a more casual manner. For a cocktail party, hors d'oeuvres may be arranged buffet-style on a sofa table.

In many homes, the living room opens directly to the dining room, making it easy to serve buffets on the table in the dining room while guests mingle in the living room. If the guests are to be seated at a table, a room divider is often used to create a more intimate environment for dining. The divider also allows you and your guests to retire to the living room afterward, leaving the cleanup for later.

(Continued)

Sit-down dinner may be served in the living room, using a folding table covered with a tablecloth.

Picnic-style entertaining on the floor in front of the fireplace is a fun approach to bad-weather days.

Coffee table and floor pillows provide a more casual alternative to the formal dining-room table.

OTHER DINING AREAS
(CONTINUED)

THE PATIO OR PORCH

The patio or porch offers a refreshing change of pace from the formal dining room. Often used for informal picnic-style dining, the patio or porch can also be used for a fancy, sunlit luncheon or for an elegant dinner at sunset.

THE TV ROOM, LIBRARY, OR DEN

The TV room has become a primary gathering place for family and friends, where snacks and light meals are frequently served in a casual, comfortable fashion. Or if you have either a library or den, you may find it a cozy setting for entertaining. For example, a few overstuffed chairs surrounding a small library table can become the perfect location for hors d'oeuvres or dessert. And, when serving a large party, consider setting up a table in the library or den, allowing the guests to separate into smaller, more intimate groups.

Porch setting (right) *provides a special atmosphere for evening entertaining.*

TV dining (below) *starts with a casual buffet service in the kitchen.*

THE BEDROOM

Breakfast in bed has long been touted as a luxurious way to begin the day. When preparing a breakfast tray, serve easy-to-eat foods, such as croissants and fresh strawberries. For a memorable event, use fancy dishes and linen napkins and add a surprise or two, like a fresh flower or a special card.

For larger breakfasts and more comfortable seating, set a small table in the bedroom. Whether you are preparing a surprise for your spouse or pampering overnight guests, a special-occasion breakfast is well worth the extra effort. The bedroom can provide a relaxed setting for that early morning cup of coffee, and guests may also appreciate a few tasty bedtime snacks.

Breakfast in the bedroom *is a special way to begin the morning. Bright colors give a cheerful, fresh look to the breakfast table.*

Jennifer and Norman

INVITATIONS

1. Come GROOVE with the Bennett's to the platinum sounds of the 1960s — ELIZABETH B

2. Saturday, Oct 20th 7:30 p.m.

3. Manchester Village East 5948 Willis Road

4. Dress appropriately in very cool duds

5. Prizes will be awarded for best outfits —

MADE IN U.S.A. FOR BENNETT ENTERPRISES INC.

A customized invitation instantly signals a special event. Creative invitations add to the anticipation of the guests, and the process of making the invitations can motivate the host and hostess in their party preparations. The style may be inspired by a party theme or by the color scheme of the table appointments.

IN ANTICIPATION of SLEEPLESS NIGHTS

Old records set the stage for a sixties theme party. Affix heavy paper to the center of the record. To mail the invitation, wrap it in brown paper or use a large padded envelope.

Diaper and T-shirt invite you to a baby shower. The details are written on the T-shirt card.

On Sunday, November 20th at 6:00 p.m.
THE PILGRIMS WILL BE GATHERING
AT THE GILBERTS' HOUSE
5960 York Avenue

Small pumpkin has the invitation for a neighborhood party written directly on it. Hand-deliver the pumpkin invitations door-to-door.

Child's handprint decorates the front of a birthday party invitation.

(Continued)

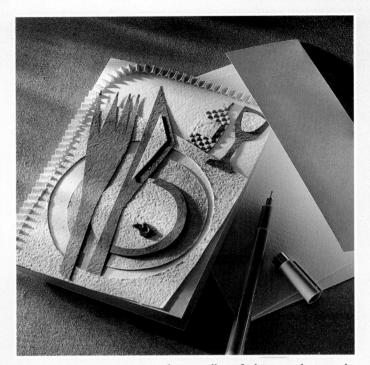

Gift wrap *a sturdy card to resemble a present. Write the invitation details on the small enclosure card.*

Paper cutouts *are arranged in a collage fashion and secured to a card with rubber cement, to make a dinner invitation.*

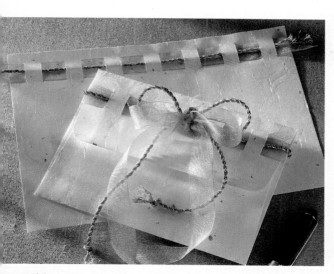

Ribbon is woven through slits, then tied in a bow, to secure the envelope of an invitation. Ribbon is also woven along one edge of the matching sheet of stationery.

Small bough of juniper is tied to the envelope of a holiday invitation with a gold ribbon. The ribbon is inserted through two slits cut in the envelope. Use a gold-ink pen to write the guests' names.

Balloon with a rolled invitation inside must be popped with a pin. Provide the pin by taping it to the balloon.

SURPRISE!

Please join us in the celebration of Alexa's 30th Birthday on Saturday, March 26th at 630 sharp 4528 Riverview South

We encourage toasting, roasting & keeping this a surprise!

THANKSGIVING DINNER

A family-style sit-down dinner often brings back many childhood memories. With a mix of heirloom and new table appointments, the traditional family dinner can take on a fresh look.

Traditional family dinner *(right) has a feeling of warmth, created by the warm colors and the varied textures of the table appointments. The richness of woods, from natural to color-washed (page 95), is combined with tapestry linens (page 49), grapevine votives (page 85), and napkin rings from miniature grapevine wreaths. A cornucopia centerpiece (page 76) completes the festive, yet homey, setting.*

Heirloom pieces *(left) mix well with current dinnerware, to evoke cherished memories of years past while giving the table a new look.*

Framed photographs *of family members serve as place cards and inspire stimulating conversation as well.*

Grapevine wreath *(left) is embellished with preserved leaves, latex fruit, and pheasant feathers, creating a seasonal wall accessory for the dining room.*

Bias swags *(page 114) are accented with bows and evergreen boughs to repeat the theme of the table setting.*

Gift-wrapped boxes *(left) are used as risers to create a tiered table setting. A wrapped box with the lid set aside holds rolled napkins tied with ribbons.*

CHRISTMAS BUFFET

The holiday season is a popular time for entertaining. Whether you are planning an open house for your friends or a Christmas Eve buffet for the family, the elegance and richness of burgundy and gold make the buffet table more festive. A combination of Christmas lights and candlelight adds a warm glow, accentuating the rich colors.

Buffet table is decorated with swagged table linens, wrapped boxes, and evergreen boughs, all accented with burgundy and gold ribbons for a coordinated setting. Christmas lights and votive candles are strewn throughout, to add a warm glow. Brass candlesticks are decorated with branches of mixed evergreens, inserted into floral foam cages as on page 73.

Wassail bowl, surrounded by a cedar wreath, is placed on a separate side table, to avoid congestion at the main buffet table. The wreath is trimmed with Christmas lights to accentuate the golden glow of the wassail.

Placemats of galax leaves and scattered flowers surround the plates. Sinamay, or angel-hair, ribbon is tied in bows around the napkins. Repeat the garden theme, using china and silverware with delicate floral patterns.

Entertain a few special friends in an elegantly appointed porch, deck, or patio setting, surrounded by nature. The garden-party theme extends to the table, dressed with fresh flowers and leaves that create tablecloths, placemats, and tray doilies. To further emphasize the garden theme, dinnerware in a floral pattern is added.

Garden setting *(left) is created with greenery and flowers at the table. A footed tray is topped with a doily of leaves arranged in a circular fashion; the tray is used for serving wrapped candies. Individual floral arrangements complete the look.*

Floral topiary *for each place setting can be easily made by inserting mini carnations into floral foam, working from the center out, then tying the stems together with a ribbon.*

Leaf tablecloth *covers a side table. Purchase galax, salal, or ti leaves from a florist; or use large leaves, such as maple, oak, or hydrangea, from your own yard. To make the tablecloth, simply glue the leaves together, using a hot glue gun.*

BACKYARD PICNIC

Access to the "great outdoors" can make summer an especially good time to entertain a large number of guests. Use casual table appointments, which are more in keeping with simple foods and a carefree, relaxed atmosphere.

To manage a large party, you may need to borrow tables and chairs from friends and neighbors, or rent them from a local church, school, or rental supply. Mismatched tables in various sizes and shapes can be unified with matching or coordinating tablecloths.

Buffet table features an assortment of baskets, used for serving the food. Votive cups, wrapped in galax leaves and raffia (page 85), hold citronella candles to repel insects. Stacked plates and cups are placed on a separate table, where a simple cotton silverware holder (page 61) organizes utensils.

Small tables, each seating four or five guests, have table toppers in assorted prints, layered over matching undercloths. At each place setting, a napkin is casually draped in a butterfly fold (page 40) and tied with sinamay ribbon. Beverage bottles filled with wildflowers are placed on each table.

Weighted corners (right) prevent tablecloths from blowing and can add a whimsical touch. For the weights, use novelty items like refrigerator magnets hung from string, fishing tackle, or mitten clips.

Entrance to the backyard is decorated with whirligigs, potted plants, and a handmade sign that welcomes the guests.

Large canopy, hung between trees and tent poles, provides shelter and shade.

AFTER-THEATER DINING

Following a special event, such as the theater or a symphony, an intimate dining experience can complete the evening in style. To give sparkle and shine, use mirrors, glass votives, and touches of gold. For high contrast, accessorize in black lacquer or ceramic. So you can enjoy being with the guests, serve finger foods and desserts that were prepared earlier.

Coffee table (right) surrounded by comfortable seating has been set with mirrors, votive candles, and cutouts from foil paper, creating high-impact sparkle. To complete the setting, bud vases are filled with elegant floral stems.

Metallic bouquets substitute for flowers. Marbles fill the vases, concealing the stems.

CHILD'S BIRTHDAY PARTY

Celebrate a child's birthday with an easy party for a few friends. Plan the party for the enjoyment of the children, focusing on activities appropriate to the birthday child's age level. For young children, be sure to plan a brief party with a small guest list.

For worry-free entertaining, set the party table in the kitchen, patio, or backyard. Inexpensive disposable table decorations minimize the workload and are just as enjoyable for the children.

Candy, crayons, and balloons *provide instant decorating for a child's party, including a potted lollipop garden, safety-lollipop napkin rings (page 99), and crayon drawings on the placemats and wall banner. As favors for the guests, balloons are tied to the chair backs, and small pails are filled with birthday treats. A new wagon, from Mom and Dad, is filled with the gifts brought to the party.*

Wall banner is started before the party. The children finish the banner with their own artwork.

Placemat borders are drawn on paper prior to the party. The young guests personalize their own placemats with original pictures.

Potted lollipops make an easy centerpiece that can be shared by the young guests. Simply fill the painted terra-cotta pots with Styrofoam®, cover the foam with Easter grass, and insert the lollipop sticks.

DINING WITH A FOREIGN FLAIR

The menu plan can often suggest a theme for the table setting, especially for an ethnic dinner. Mexican and Italian menus may suggest colorful buffet-style dinners with lots of menu items to choose from. An Oriental menu may inspire you to seat guests around a low table on floor pillows so they can use chopsticks or enjoy a tea ceremony.

Party Italian Style
May 28 7:00 p.m.
Grazie!

Italian buffet *features small Italian flags and red, green, and white table runners. A red-and-white checked design is painted on an old wooden tray to resemble a checked napkin, and grapevine garland is arranged on the table. The name of each entrée is written on an uncooked lasagna noodle placed next to the serving piece. To carry out the theme, use wines from Italy, jars filled with spaghetti, old bricks to serve as risers, and green glassware.*

*Everything from mild to hot...
A Mexican fiesta that will
give your chip a reason to dip.
Food and entertainment until midnight.*

Mexican buffet *features large terra-cotta saucers as serving trays, colorful paper plates used on basket liners, napkin rings embellished with worry dolls, tinware, maracas, and an old Mexican minichair. Jalapeño and bell peppers, like the fresh fruit centerpiece on page 78, are arranged on a footed stand.*

Oriental setting *is created with a coffee table and floor seating on pillows. Rice paper, torn into rectangles, is used to make the placemats, and palm leaves are wrapped around the chopsticks. The dinnerware and napkins reflect the Oriental theme, and a bonsai tree is added to the table arrangement.*

THE ORIENT EXPRESS WILL BE STOPPING IN OUR LIVINGROOM ON THURSDAY, AUGUST 25 AT 6 PM

HANDS ON ... NO CUTLERY

Table
Linens

BASIC TABLE LINENS

For variety, make a selection of basic tablecloths, including round, square, and oval styles, as well as placemats and napkins in several colors. By sewing your own tablecloths, you can make custom sizes and shapes for nonstandard tables, including oval tables.

For table linens, you may want to select durable, stain-resistant decorator fabrics that have been treated to repel soil and water. To avoid seaming large tablecloths, choose a wide fabric, such as one of the 72" (183 cm) tablecloth linens available at fabric stores. Or gain the extra width needed by adding a border to the tablecloth as on pages 49 to 51. Round tablecloths are frequently seamed, but the seam falls into the drape of the fabric along one side of the tablecloth, making it less noticeable.

For a greater selection of wide tablecloth fabrics, you can recut a ready-made purchased tablecloth to fit the actual size and shape of your table, instead of using a purchased fabric.

Determine the length and width of the tablecloth by measuring across the tabletop in both directions. Then add twice the desired *drop length,* or overhang, to this measurement. Drop lengths range from 8" (20.5 cm) to floor-length, with most drop lengths between 10" and 15" (25.5 and 38 cm).

Placemats range in size from 12" × 17" (30.5 × 43 cm) to 14" × 19" (35.5 × 48.5 cm). Finish them with a simple hem or edge finish as on pages 38 and 39. Or, for a more decorative look, select from the styles on pages 49 and 56.

Make napkins in a generous size, such as 15" (38 cm) square for luncheon napkins and 18" (46 cm) square for dinner napkins. Generously sized napkins offer liberal protection for the guests, and many napkin-folding techniques (page 40) are more successful with the larger sizes.

All that is needed to make basic tablecloths, placemats, and napkins is to finish the edges. For simplicity, press a narrow hem in place, mitering the corners of squares and rectangles, and stitch the hem on the conventional sewing machine. Or finish the edges of the table linens with the 3-thread overlock stitch on a serger.

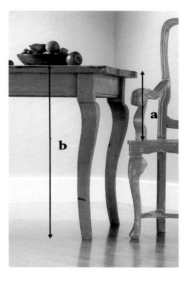

Drop length is the distance you want the tablecloth to hang over the edge of the table. Determine the exact drop length for your table by measuring. You may want the tablecloth to clear the chair seats and hang freely **(a);** this drop length will measure from 8" to 10" (20.5 to 25.5 cm). For a more formal look, use a longer drop length. Floor-length tablecloths **(b)** and tablecloths that drape onto the floor are especially elegant.

HOW TO CUT A ROUND TABLECLOTH

1 Measure the diameter of the round table; add twice the drop length, to determine the measurement for the finished tablecloth. Cut a square of fabric at least 1" (2.5 cm) larger than this size; piece two fabric widths together, if necessary, and press seam open. Fold square of fabric in half lengthwise and crosswise. Pin layers together.

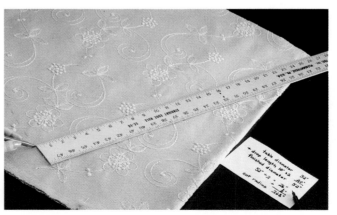

2 Divide measurement for the finished tablecloth by two and add ½" (1.3 cm), to determine radius of cut circle. Mark an arc, using straightedge and pencil, measuring from the folded center of fabric, a distance equal to radius. Cut on marked line through all layers.

HOW TO CUT AN OVAL OR CUSTOM-SHAPED TABLECLOTH

1 Measure the length and width of table at longest points; add twice the drop length. Cut a rectangle of fabric at least 1" (2.5 cm) larger than this size; piece the fabric widths together, if necessary, and press the seams open.

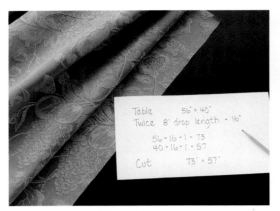

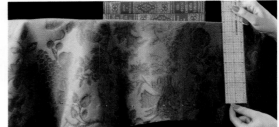

2 Place fabric on table, centered lengthwise and crosswise; weight fabric down. Measure and mark around tablecloth, an amount equal to the desired drop length plus ½" (1.3 cm). Cut on the marked line.

HOW TO NARROW-HEM TABLE LINENS USING THE CONVENTIONAL SEWING MACHINE

CUTTING DIRECTIONS

Cut the tablecloth, placemat, or napkin 1" (2.5 cm) larger than the desired finished size, piecing fabric widths together, if necessary, for large tablecloths.

1 **Rectangular or square linens.** Press under ½" (1.3 cm) on each side of fabric. Unfold corner; fold diagonally so pressed folds match. Press the diagonal fold; trim corner as shown.

2 Fold under the raw edge ¼" (6 mm). Press double-fold hem in place.

3 Stitch the hem close to inner fold, using straight stitch on conventional sewing machine and pivoting at corners; do not stitch along folds of miter.

1 **Round or oval linens.** Stitch around fabric circle or oval, a scant ¼" (6 mm) from raw edge. Fold and press the fabric along stitching line.

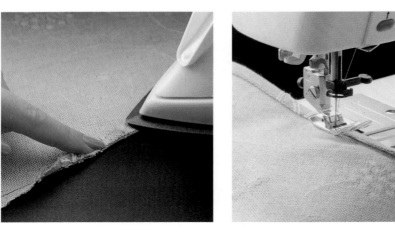

2 Fold and press fabric again to make a ¼" (6 mm) double-fold hem, easing in excess fabric. Stitch hem close to inner fold, using straight stitch on conventional machine.

HOW TO EDGE-FINISH TABLE LINENS USING A SERGER

1 Rectangular or square linens.
Set the serger for balanced 3-thread overlock stitch, threading both the loopers of machine with woolly nylon thread, if desired, for best thread coverage; use regular thread in needle. Set the stitch width at 4 to 5 mm; set stitch length at 1 mm. Check the stitch quality on a sample of fabric; adjust the tension, if necessary.

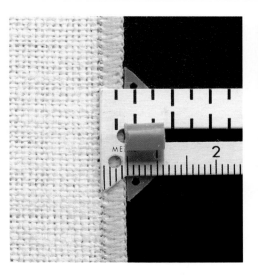

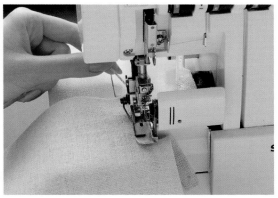

2 Stitch along one side of fabric, then opposite side, holding the tail chain taut as you begin stitching; trim away ½" (1.3 cm) with serger blade. Leave long tail chain at ends.

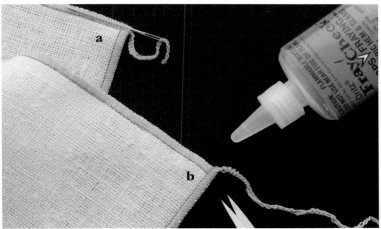

3 Stitch remaining two sides of fabric as in step 2. Thread the tail chain through eye of tapestry needle, and weave needle under overlock stitches for about 1" (2.5 cm) **(a)**; cut off remaining length of tail chain. Or apply liquid fray preventer to stitches at corners **(b)**; allow to dry, and cut off entire tail chain.

1 Round or oval linens. Set serger as in step 1, above. Stitch around the tablecloth, trimming ½" (1.3 cm) with the serger blade; at beginning, stitch onto edge of fabric at an angle.

2 Overlap the previous stitches for 1" (2.5 cm) at end. Lift presser foot, and shift fabric so it is behind needle. Stitch straight off edge of the fabric as shown; continue stitching to leave a long tail chain. (Presser foot was removed to show needle position.)

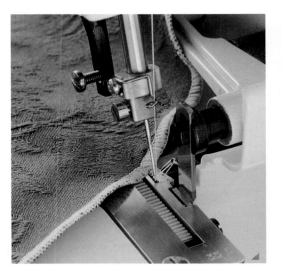

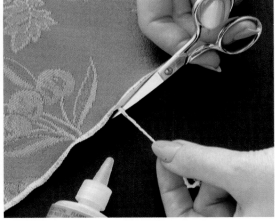

3 Apply liquid fray preventer to tail chain. Trim tail chain next to stitches.

NAPKIN FOLDS

For added flair at sit-down dinners and buffets, fold the dinner napkins in an interesting way. Try different napkin folds for different occasions, to continually vary the look of the table setting. Included on the following pages are several tailored restaurant-style folds, softer fan-fold and butterfly-fold styles, and dinnerware holders.

Fleur-de-lis fold

Bishop's-hat fold

Butterfly fold

Horizontal-fold dinnerware holder

Wineglass fan fold

Tabletop fan fold

Mitered stand

Flipped-points fold

Tiered-points fold

Diagonal-fold dinnerware holder

1 **Bishop's-hat fold.** Fold napkin in half diagonally, right side out, with the fold at the bottom.

2 Bring up the two bottom points to meet the top point.

3 Fold up the lower point of the napkin to 1" (2.5 cm) below the top point.

4 Fold down the lower point of the napkin to meet the bottom fold.

5 Curve sides to back, and tuck one side into the other (right), forming a circular base; stand upright. This completes the Bishop's-hat napkin fold, as shown from the front (left).

Fleur-de-lis fold. Follow steps 1 to 5, above. Fold down the two front points, to make fleur-de-lis napkin fold.

THE MITERED STAND

1 Fold the napkin in half diagonally, right side out, with the fold at the bottom.

2 Bring up two bottom points to meet top point.

3 Fold down the top half of the napkin, toward the back.

4 Fold napkin in half again, standing napkin upright.

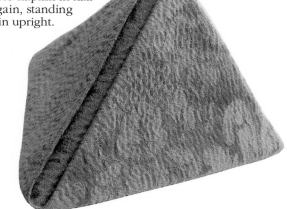

THE BUTTERFLY FOLD

2 Fold napkin in half at pleated center; insert the center of the napkin into napkin ring, allowing both sides of napkin to flair out gracefully.

1 Place napkin, right side up, on table. Accordion-pleat fabric by hand, diagonally from corner to corner.

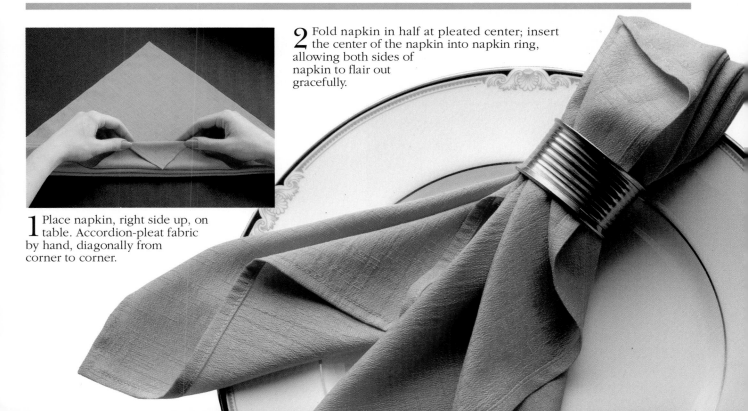

THE TABLETOP FAN FOLD

1 Fold napkin in half, right side out, with fold at the top. Accordion-pleat across the napkin for three-fourths the length, folding the first pleat down.

2 End pleating with pleats on bottom, next to table, and the unpleated section to the right. Fold top half of the napkin over the bottom half.

3 Hold the napkin upright, with open end of the pleats pointing upward.

4 Fold the unpleated section of the napkin diagonally to form a stand; tuck in stand as shown, and allow pleats to fan out.

THE TIERED-POINTS FOLD

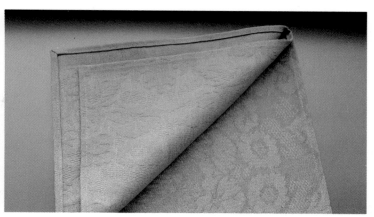

1 Fold napkin in half, right side out, with fold at top; then fold in half again, with corners of the napkin at lower right.

2 Fold back first layer of napkin diagonally so corner is at upper left. Fold back second layer to 1" (2.5 cm) from first corner.

4 Fold sides under. Place napkin flat on the table.

3 Repeat with third and fourth layers, so all corners of napkin are spaced 1" (2.5 cm) apart.

THE WINEGLASS FAN FOLD

2 Place folded lower edge of the napkin into goblet, allowing top of napkin to fan out.

1 Fold napkin in half, right side up, with fold at bottom. Accordion-fold across napkin, from side to side, folding the first and last pleats down.

THE FLIPPED-POINTS FOLD

1 Fold napkin in half, right side out, with fold at bottom; then fold in half again, with corners of napkin at upper right. Fold back first layer of napkin diagonally so corner is at lower left.

2 Fold back second layer of napkin so corner touches the center fold. Bring first corner of napkin from lower left to meet second corner at center fold.

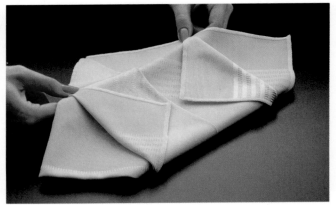

3 Fold under the sides of the napkin, folding napkin into thirds. Place flat on table in vertical position.

THE HORIZONTAL-FOLD DINNERWARE HOLDER

1 Fold napkin in half, wrong side out, with the fold at the bottom.

THE DIAGONAL-FOLD DINNERWARE HOLDER

1 Fold the napkin in half, right side out, with the fold at bottom; then fold in half again, with corners of napkin at upper right.

2 Fold down the first layer of the napkin 2" (5 cm).

3 Fold same corner over itself two times, creating a diagonal band across napkin.

4 Fold down the second layer of the napkin, tucking the corner into diagonal band and creating a second band, 1" (2.5 cm) wide.

5 Fold under the top and bottom of napkin, folding napkin into thirds. Place flat on table, turning the napkin into vertical position, with folds on the diagonal.

2 Fold one-third of top layer of napkin down, forming a center band.

3 Turn the napkin over. Fold sides in to meet at center back; fold together.

Placemat combines two coordinating tapestry fabrics and features border strips at the sides.

TAPESTRY TABLE LINENS

Tapestry fabrics add simple elegance to table settings. Because tapestries often have intricate patterns, they work best for table linens of a straightforward design, such as the bordered tablecloths and placemats shown here. To simplify the construction and prevent excessive bulk at the edges, the tapestry tablecoverings are lined to the edge.

Select two coordinating tapestry fabrics, one for the center portion and one for the border strips. To reduce bulk, use muslin for the lining, or select a lightweight cotton in a color that matches the border fabric.

Tablecloth shows off a wide border, mitered at the corners.

Determine the size of the center panel and the borders, based on your personal preference and on the design in the fabric you have selected. Because tapestries usually shrink a significant amount, steam press both the fabrics before cutting the pieces.

MATERIALS

- Two coordinating tapestry fabrics.
- Muslin or other lightweight cotton, for lining.

HOW TO SEW
A BORDERED TAPESTRY PLACEMAT

CUTTING DIRECTIONS

Determine the finished length and width of the placemat; placemats range in size from 12" × 17" (30.5 × 43 cm) to 14" × 19" (35.5 × 48.5 cm). To determine the cut size of the middle panel from side to side, subtract two times the desired finished width of the border; then add 1" (2.5 cm) to allow for two ½" (1.3 cm) seam allowances. The cut size of the middle panel from front to back is 1" (2.5 cm) longer than the desired finished size.

Cut two border strips, each 1" (2.5 cm) wider than the desired finished width of the border and 1" (2.5 cm) longer than the desired finished size of the placemat from front to back.

Cut the lining as in step 2, below, after the border has been applied.

1 Stitch border strips to the sides of middle panel, stitching ½" (1.3 cm) seams. Press seams open.

2 Cut the lining ¼" (6 mm) shorter than length and width of pieced top; this prevents the lining from showing on the right side at edges.

(Continued)

3 Pin the lining to the pieced top, right sides together, matching raw edges. With lining side up, stitch ½" (1.3 cm) seam on all four sides, taking one diagonal stitch across corners; leave an opening on one side for turning.

4 Trim seam allowances diagonally across the corners; apply liquid fray preventer. Press the lining seam allowance toward lining. Turn right side out; press. Hand-stitch opening closed.

HOW TO SEW A BORDERED TAPESTRY TABLECLOTH

CUTTING DIRECTIONS

Determine the finished length and width of the tablecloth, including the drop length, as on page 37. To determine the cut size of the middle panel, subtract two times the desired finished width of the border from the finished length and width of the tablecloth; then add 1" (2.5 cm), to allow for ½" (1.3 cm) seam allowances.

You will need four border strips, with the cut width equal to the desired finished width of the border plus 1" (2.5 cm). To determine the length of the border strips, add two times the cut width of the border plus 2" (5 cm) to the cut side of the middle panel; cut two border strips based on the width of the middle panel and cut two based on the length of the middle panel.

Cut the lining as in step 9, opposite, after the border has been applied.

1 Mark middle panel at center of each side, on wrong side; mark center of each border strip on wrong side.

2 Mark the middle panel at all corners, ½" (1.3 cm) from each raw edge, on wrong side of fabric.

3 Pin one border strip to one side of middle panel, right sides together, matching raw edges and centers.

4 Stitch border strip to middle panel in ½" (1.3 cm) seam, starting and ending at corner markings.

5 Fold middle panel diagonally at corners, matching border seams and raw edges of border strips. Place a straightedge along the fold; draw stitching line for mitered seam on border, using chalk. Stitching line should be at 45° angle to raw edge.

6 Pin and stitch mitered seam, beginning at raw edge and ending at previous seamline.

7 Trim the seam allowances on mitered corners to ½" (1.3 cm). Trim the middle panel diagonally across corners of border seam. Apply liquid fray preventer to trimmed edges, to prevent raveling.

8 Clip the seam allowances of border strips at corners. Apply liquid fray preventer. Press all seams open.

9 Cut the lining ½" (1.3 cm) shorter than the length and width of the pieced top; this prevents the lining from showing on the right side at the edges. Finish tablecloth as for placemat, steps 3 and 4, opposite.

BULLION FRINGE TABLE LINENS

Bullion fringe adds elegance to table linens. It may be stitched around the edges of tablecloths or along the short, angled ends of a table runner. Bullion fringe is available in acetate, rayon, cotton, and metallic as well as in a variety of fringe lengths. Because the heading of the fringe ravels quickly, always apply liquid fray preventer to the area that will be cut and allow it to dry before cutting the fringe.

Round tablecloth *has a luxurious look when trimmed with bullion fringe. At left, an oversized tablecloth falls elegantly onto the floor.*

Table runner with fringed ends drapes gracefully over the table. The ends of the table runner are angled to add interest.

Small square tablecloth with bullion fringe edging is placed on the table at an angle.

HOW TO SEW A ROUND TABLECLOTH WITH BULLION FRINGE

1 Determine desired drop length for the tablecloth; subtract length of fringe, excluding the heading. Add twice this measurement to diameter of the round tabletop, to determine the diameter of fabric circle. Cut a square of fabric at least this size; piece two fabric widths together, if necessary, and press seam open. Fold square of fabric in half lengthwise and crosswise. Pin layers together.

2 Divide measurement for diameter of fabric circle by two, to determine radius. Mark an arc, using straightedge and pencil, measuring from folded center of fabric, a distance equal to radius. Cut on marked line through all layers.

3 Stitch around outer edge of fabric circle, using zigzag or overlock stitch; if using overlock stitch, do not trim edge of fabric. Pin the bullion fringe to fabric, with bottom of heading along edge of fabric; steam press as necessary to shape heading around curve.

4 Fold under ¾" (2 cm) at ends of heading; butt folded ends. Straight-stitch along top and bottom of heading.

HOW TO SEW A RECTANGULAR OR SQUARE TABLECLOTH WITH BULLION FRINGE

1 Determine the desired drop length for the tablecloth; subtract length of fringe, excluding the heading. Add twice this measurement to length and width of the tabletop, to determine cut size of fabric. Piece the fabric widths together, if necessary, and press seams open.

2 Stitch around all edges of the fabric, using zigzag or overlock stitch; if using overlock stitch, do not trim edge of fabric. Pin bullion fringe to fabric, with bottom of heading along edge of fabric, starting at middle of one side.

HOW TO SEW A TABLE RUNNER WITH BULLION FRINGE

1 Determine the cut length of the table runner as for length of rectangular tablecloth, step 1, opposite. Cut a rectangle from the face fabric, 16" (40.5 cm) wide and to determined cut length; cut rectangle from the lining, 15¾" (40 cm) wide and to the same length as the face fabric. Pin the rectangles, right sides together, matching the raw edges on the long sides. Stitch ½" (1.3 cm) on long edges. Turn right side out; press.

2 Mark one end of runner on long and short sides, 5" (25.5 cm) from corners. Draw lines diagonally across corners, between the marked points. Trim on marked lines. Repeat for other end of runner. Serge or zigzag layers together.

3 Pin the bullion fringe to the short ends, with the bottom of the heading along edge of fabric. Shape heading at corners, easing in fullness.

4 Fold under ¾" (2 cm) at ends of heading. Straight-stitch along top and bottom of heading, pivoting at corners.

3 Miter corners by tucking excess heading on left side of corner under the fold in the heading on right side; this will keep the heading from catching in the toes of presser foot as you sew.

4 Fold under ¾" (2 cm) at ends of heading; butt the folded ends. Straight-stitch along the top and bottom of heading. Turn the handwheel manually to stitch over the thick areas at folded ends and corners.

HEXAGONAL PLACEMATS

H exagonal in shape, these placemats are a welcome change of pace from the usual rectangular placemats. Mitered braid or ribbon adds a simple border on the pointed sides, calling attention to the unique shape of the placemat.

For a coordinated look, use these placemats with triangle-point valances (page 118) in the dining room. Buttons and tassels may be added to the center points at the sides as a finishing touch.

HOW TO SEW A HEXAGONAL PLACEMAT

MATERIALS (for four placemats)

- 1 yd. (0.95 m) fabric, for placemat tops.
- 1 yd. (0.95 m) fabric, for placemat backs.
- 4½ yd. (4.15 m) braid, grosgrain ribbon, or other tightly woven flat trim.
- Two buttons and two tassels for each placemat, if desired.

CUTTING DIRECTIONS

Make the pattern for the placemat as in step 1. For each placemat, cut one placemat top and one placemat back, using the pattern. Steam press the trim to preshrink it; cut two 20" (51 cm) lengths.

1 Draw 15" × 23" (38 × 58.5 cm) rectangle. Mark center of each short side. On long sides, mark points 5" (12.5 cm) from the corners. Draw the cutting lines from center marks on short sides to marked points on long sides. Cut pattern.

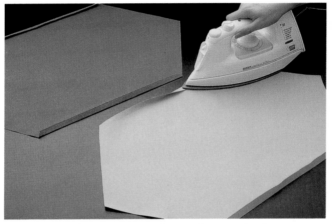

2 Cut one placemat top and one placemat back, using pattern. Press under ½" (1.3 cm) on upper and lower edges of both pieces.

3 Pin placemat top and placemat back, right sides together, along pointed sides, matching raw edges; align folds on upper and lower edges. Stitch ½" (1.3 cm) seams on pointed sides.

4 Clip diagonally across corner. Press the seam allowances of the placemat back toward placemat back. Turn right side out, and press seamed edges.

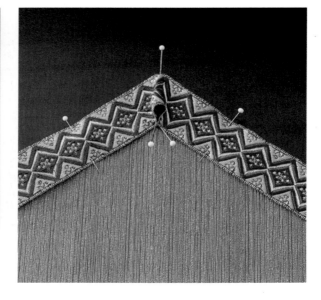

5 Pin the trim to sides of placemat top, matching outer edges of trim and placemat. At points, mark the trim at edges, for miters.

6 Remove trim. With trim folded right sides together, stitch miters from mark at inner corner to mark at outer edge.

7 Trim mitered seam to ¼" (6 mm), leaving the outer point untrimmed.

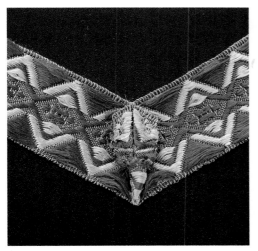

8 Press the seam open, and press the point flat.

9 Pin trim to placemat top. Fold ends at upper and lower edges between placemat top and placemat back; press.

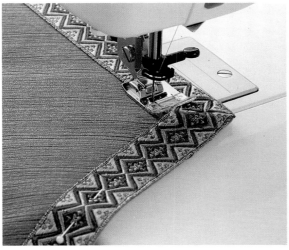

10 Pin placemat top and placemat back together along the upper and lower edges. Edgestitch around entire placemat, stitching trims in place. Edgestitch along inner edges of trims.

11 Stitch buttons at points of trim, if desired. Secure the loop of the tassel around the button.

SILVERWARE HOLDERS

Neatly arrange the silverware at a buffet in a silverware holder. The holder, either with or without lace trim, is divided into twenty-four compartments that separate the silverware for each guest. Constructed from four layered semicircles of fabric, the holder has radiating stitching lines that divide it into eighths, creating three rows of silverware compartments. For silverware with heavy handles, divide the holder into sixths instead of eighths, making eighteen larger compartments.

MATERIALS

- ¾ yd. (0.7 m) fabric.
- 6½ yd. (5.95 m) gathered lace trim. 2½" to 3" (6.5 to 7.5 cm) wide, optional.

Silverware holder *may have a simple, tailored look as shown above. Or, for a more Victorian look, add lace trim as shown at left.*

HOW TO MAKE A SILVERWARE HOLDER
WITH LACE TRIM

1 Draw four semicircles on tracing paper, one each with a radius of 6", 8", 10", and 12" (15, 20.5, 25.5, and 30.5 cm). On the straight sides, add ½" (1.3 cm) seam allowance. Cut one semicircle of each size from fabric. The pieces will be referred to as A, B, C, and D, from the smallest to the largest.

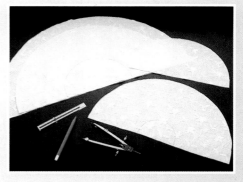

2 Mark all fabric pieces on center of each straight side. On Piece B, lightly mark an arc 2" (5 cm) from center point; on Piece C, lightly mark an arc 4" (10 cm) from center point.

(Continued)

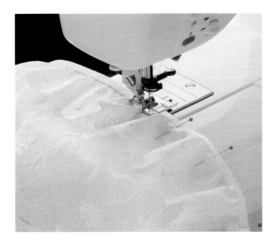

3 Pin lace trim to curved edge of Pieces A, B, and C, with right sides together and gathered edge of the lace along outer edge of fabric; match ends of lace trim to straight side of semicircle. Stitch just inside the gathered heading of lace trim.

4 Turn lace right side up; press seam allowances toward fabric. From the right side, topstitch ⅛" (3 mm) from seamline.

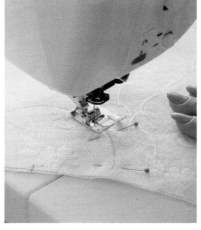

5 Repeat steps 3 and 4 for Piece D, folding a narrow double-fold hem at ends of the lace; begin and end the lace trim ½" (1.3 cm) from straight edge of semicircle.

6 Place Piece B over Piece C, right sides up, with straight edges even and matching center points. Pin and stitch along marked arc on Piece B.

7 Place Piece A over Piece B, right sides up, with the straight edges even and matching center points. Place Piece D over Piece A, right side up, with straight edges even and matching center points. Pin through all layers along straight edge.

8 Stitch ½" (1.3 cm) seam on the straight side. Press the seam open.

9 Turn Piece D to the back of the silverware holder; press in place.

10 Fold back the top two layers to reveal the marked arc on Piece C; pin along arc through bottom two layers. Stitch along arc, beginning and ending at lower seam; take care not to catch top two layers in stitching.

11 Fold pattern for Piece D in half, then into quarters and eighths. Transfer the markings from the pattern to Piece D, using pins. This marks the dividing lines for the silverware compartments.

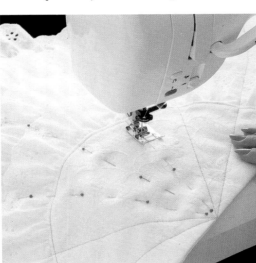

12 Stitch along the first marked line from the outer edge to the center point. Pivot at center point and stitch back to the outer edge along the opposite marked line. Repeat for two more sets of pressed lines. Stitch the last marked line from center point to outer edge.

13 Embellish the center point of the holder as desired with a bow, lace motif, or flowers. Insert silverware into layered compartments.

HOW TO MAKE A SILVERWARE HOLDER WITHOUT LACE TRIM

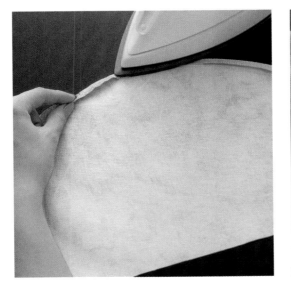

1 Follow steps 1 and 2 on page 61, except cut 8", 10", 12", and 14" (20.5, 25.5, 30.5, and 35.5 cm) semicircles. Stitch along the curved edges of all the semicircles, using overlock or zigzag stitch; press under ¼" (6 mm), and topstitch in place.

2 Follow steps 6 to 13, opposite. Clip the seam allowance on Piece D next to curved edge of Piece C; fold to the back, and hem.

TRAY DOILIES

For a custom look, make a lace-trimmed doily to fit a silver, brass, or wooden serving tray. Select fine linen or cotton fabric for a crisp doily that launders well. When selecting lace trim for an oval or round doily, keep in mind that narrow laces and laces with scallops or points on the outer edge are easier to shape around curves.

MATERIALS

- Lightweight linen or cotton fabric.
- Flat lace edging with one straight and one scalloped edge; allow extra yardage for shaping along curves or mitering corners.

HOW TO SEW A TRAY DOILY WITH CURVED SIDES

1 Place tracing paper over the tray; trace around rim of the tray with a pencil, to make pattern. Using pattern, cut fabric to finished size of doily.

2 Sew a gathering row along the straight edge of lace, if lace does not have a gathering thread in the heading.

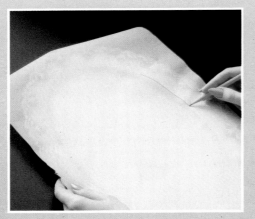

3 Pin the lace edging to the doily fabric, aligning outer edge of lace to the outer edge of fabric. Pull the gathering thread to shape the inner edge of lace around the curve; overlap the ends of lace ⅜" (1 cm). Steam press.

4 Stitch along the inner, straight edge of lace, beginning at the center of the overlap, using narrow zigzag stitch.

5 Trim the fabric underneath the lace, ⅛" (3 mm) from stitching. At the overlap, stitch through both layers of lace, and trim excess lace close to stitching.

HOW TO SEW A TRAY DOILY WITH STRAIGHT SIDES

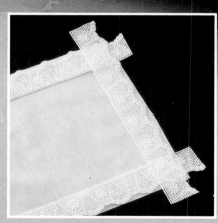

1 Make pattern and cut fabric for a tray with straight sides, such as a rectangular tray, as in step 1, opposite. Plan the lace placement so corners will miter attractively; it may not be possible to miter all corners alike.

2 Cut the lace edging into lengths slightly longer than each side. Pin lace edging to doily fabric, aligning the outer edge of the lace to the outer edge of the fabric.

3 Stitch along inner, straight edges of lace, using narrow zigzag. Trim the fabric underneath the lace. Stitch through both layers of lace from inner corner to outer corner; trim excess lace close to the stitching.

Lighted glass-top table *is created by placing a lamp with a globe bulb under the table. The light adds a warm glow to the layered tablecloths of cotton and lace.*

Heavy woven rug, *used instead of a traditional tablecloth, adds rich texture to a table setting.*

Battenberg lace *is draped softly over risers. Used over a damask tablecloth with bullion fringe (page 52), this elegant lace makes a dessert buffet extra special.*

Mexican blanket *is arranged artfully to add emphasis to a display of pottery and baskets, creating a focal point on a buffet table.*

Table runners *from two different fabrics are woven together to create a unique table covering.*

Table
Accessories

DECORATING WITH
FRESH FLOWERS

Fresh flowers add a luxurious quality to the table. Hand-picked from your own garden or purchased from the florist, fresh flowers can be easily arranged, following a few simple tips. They can be displayed as candlestick arrangements (page 72) or table wreaths (page 74) and in many other creative ways (page 80).

The long-lasting flowers listed below are excellent choices for table arrangements at dinner parties, because they can be arranged ahead of time. If the arrangement will be made in advance, select compact blossoms.

Every day, replace the water in the container with fresh water and mist the blossoms in the arrangement to increase the freshness time. Do not, however, mist the blossoms of orchids and succulents, because misting them causes brown spots.

TIPS FOR USING FRESH FLOWERS

Hammer the stems of woody plants, such as yarrow, forsythia, and blossoming tree branches, for 1½" to 2" (3.8 to 5 cm), to increase water absorption; for sunflowers, hammer stems lightly.

Cut the stems of most fresh flowers on the diagonal, using sharp knife, to increase water absorption. Snap stems of chrysanthemums.

Remove pollen from lilies by pulling out the stamens. Falling pollen discolors the petals of the lilies and stains table linens and clothing.

Cut stems of roses under water and on the diagonal, about 2" (5 cm) from the end, using a sharp knife. When stems are not cut under water, air bubbles form at the ends of stems, preventing water from rising up the stems.

LONG-LASTING FRESH FLOWERS

VARIETY	AVAILABLE COLORS	LASTING TIME
ALLIUM	Purple and white	10 to 12 days
ALSTROEMERIA	Many colors	8 to 10 days
ASTER	Purple and white	8 to 10 days
BABY'S BREATH	White	7 to 14 days
CARNATION	Many colors	7 to 14 days
CHRYSANTHEMUM	Many colors	10 to 12 days
CORNFLOWER	Blue and pink	8 to 10 days
FORSYTHIA	Yellow	12 to 14 days
FREESIA	Yellow, pink, purple, and white	5 to 7 days
FRUIT-TREE BLOSSOM	Many colors	10 to 14 days
GINGERROOT HELICONIA	Red and pink	8 to 10 days
HEATHER	Purple and mauve	10 to 14 days
LIATRIS	Purple and white	7 to 10 days
LILY	Many colors	7 to 10 days
ORCHIDS	Many colors	5 to 10 days
ROSE	Many colors	5 to 7 days
STAR-OF-BETHLEHEM	White	10 to 14 days
STATICE	Many colors	14 to 21 days
SUNFLOWER	Yellow with brown	14 to 21 days
YARROW	White and yellow	10 to 14 days

CANDLESTICK FLORAL ARRANGEMENTS

Fresh flowers, brass candlesticks, and tall tapers add grace and elegance to a formal table setting. Made from roses, star-of-Bethlehem, leatherleaf fern, caspia, and cornflowers, these candlestick arrangements are delicate and colorful. Different varieties of floral materials may be substituted, keeping the scale of the arrangement in mind.

MATERIALS

- Brass candlestick and taper candle.

- Roses; star-of-Bethlehem; leatherleaf fern; caspia; cornflowers.

- Floral foam cage, such as Oasis® Iglu™ holder for fresh flowers; plastic candle holder.

- Floral adhesive clay; 24-gauge floral wire; wire cutter.

HOW TO MAKE A CANDLESTICK FLORAL ARRANGEMENT

1 Apply floral adhesive clay to rim of the candlestick.

2 Soak floral foam cage in water until saturated; wire the cage to the top of candlestick, using 24-gauge floral wire.

3 Trim edges of plastic candle holder; insert candle holder into center of foam cage.

4 Cut the stems of the roses 1" to 1½" (2.5 to 3.8 cm) long, cutting diagonally under water with sharp knife. Insert stems into floral foam, spacing them evenly.

5 Cut star-of-Bethlehem stems 1" to 1½" (2.5 to 3.8 cm) long, cutting them diagonally with sharp knife. Insert stems into floral foam, spacing evenly. Allow some to drape downward.

7 Mist the arrangement with water; wipe the candlestick dry. Insert a candle.

6 Cut stems of leatherleaf fern, caspia, and cornflowers diagonally; insert into foam, filling any bare areas with fern and caspia and adding accents of cornflowers.

FRESH FLORAL TABLE WREATHS

Floral centerpieces add color and life to any table setting. This table wreath is easily assembled by simply covering a foam wreath form with greenery, then inserting floral stems into the foam. Displayed with pillar candles in the center, the wreath makes an impressive arrangement for a dining-room table or buffet. Floral varieties other than those shown here may be used to suit your preferences.

MATERIALS

- Ivy.
- Honeysuckle vines.
- Roses.
- Freesia.
- Statice.
- Smilax garland.
- Leatherleaf fern.
- Sheet moss.
- Foam wreath form for fresh flowers; floral pins.
- Grouping of pillar candles to fit within the center of wreath form.

HOW TO MAKE A FRESH FLORAL TABLE WREATH

1 Soak foam wreath form in water until saturated; dampen the sheet moss. Cover wreath form with sheet moss; secure with floral pins.

2 Drape ivy stems over the wreath; secure with floral pins. Insert stems of leatherleaf fern into wreath; cut small openings in moss with a knife, if necessary, so stems can be inserted easily.

3 Cut honeysuckle vine into desired lengths. Insert both ends into the foam, maintaining curve of the vine and spacing vines randomly.

4 Cut stems of roses about 2" (5 cm) long, cutting them diagonally under water with sharp knife. Insert the stems into floral foam, spacing them evenly.

5 Cut stems of freesia about 2" (5 cm) long, cutting them diagonally with a sharp knife. Insert into floral foam, spacing them evenly. Repeat for statice, filling any bare areas.

6 Mist the wreath with water; place on layers of newspaper for several hours, to soak up excess water; or display the wreath on a platter. Place grouping of pillar candles in center of wreath.

DRIED CORNUCOPIA
CENTERPIECES

For an autumn feast, a cornucopia overflowing with dried naturals is a classic centerpiece. From the dozens of dried varieties available, select several, in a range of colors, shapes, and textures.

For a unique arrangement, consider using preserved roses, wheat, nigella pods, and yarrow instead of the more traditional gourds and Indian corn. For even more contrast in texture, accent the dried naturals with latex fruits.

To assemble the arrangement, fill the cornucopia with floral foam covered with moss. Then insert the dried naturals into the foam, one layer at a time.

MATERIALS

- Wicker cornucopia.
- Floral foam for dried arranging; sheet moss.
- Preserved autumn leaves; dried naturals, such as preserved roses, wheat, nigella pods, and yarrow.
- Latex or other artificial fruit, such as apples, grapes, and berries.
- 20-gauge floral wire; U-shaped floral pins; wired floral picks; hot glue gun and glue sticks.

HOW TO MAKE A DRIED CORNUCOPIA CENTERPIECE

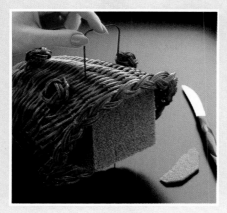

1 Cut a piece of floral foam to fit inside cornucopia, using serrated knife. Insert wire through bottom of basket, then through foam.

2 Place a small piece of folded paper or cardboard on top of the foam, between wire ends; twist wire ends tightly over paper. This prevents wire from tearing the foam.

3 Cover foam loosely with moss; pin in place as necessary, using floral pins.

4 Insert the stems of the preserved leaves into the foam so leaves rest on table. Insert bunch of one type of dried naturals, such as nigella pods, into foam next to the leaves.

5 Insert cluster of latex grapes or other fruit on one side of the arrangement, above leaves. Wrap the wire from a floral pick around several stems of wheat; insert the pick into the foam near the center of arrangement, above leaves.

6 Insert several stems of roses in a cluster, next to grapes. Insert clusters of each remaining material, such as yarrow, arranging one variety at a time.

7 Fill in any bare areas with additional leaves or small grape clusters. Use hot glue, if necessary, to secure any individual items, such as single leaves, that cannot be inserted into foam.

FRESH FRUIT CENTERPIECES

A cake stand is used as the base for this appealing table arrangement of fresh fruit, adding height and drama. A wide variety of fruits is used in the centerpiece, and, for even more visual interest, honeysuckle vines and fresh greenery are added.

MATERIALS

- Fresh fruit, including apples, pears, oranges, bananas, and grapes.
- Footed cake stand.
- Honeysuckle vines; fresh galax leaves.
- Filler materials, such as yarrow, ming fern, and salal leaves.
- Wired ribbon.
- Styrofoam® ball, 6" (15 cm) in diameter.
- Floral adhesive clay.
- Wooden skewers or picks; wired floral picks.

HOW TO MAKE A FRESH FRUIT CENTERPIECE

1 Cut Styrofoam ball in half; secure to top of cake stand with floral adhesive clay.

2 Insert honeysuckle vines into Styrofoam, allowing some vines to cascade around base of cake stand.

3 Insert wooden skewers or picks into apples 1" to 2" (2.5 to 5 cm). Secure to the Styrofoam, grouping apples closely on one side of the arrangement. Break off ends of skewers or picks if they are too long.

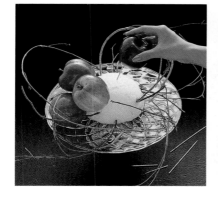

4 Secure pears on side opposite the apples, using wooden skewers or picks. Secure two clusters of oranges on opposite sides of the arrangement, between the apples and the pears.

5 Wrap wire from one floral pick around small cluster of bananas; insert floral pick into the Styrofoam, allowing bananas to cascade downward over the rim of cake stand. Repeat for cluster of bananas on the opposite side.

6 Wrap wire from one floral pick around two or three stems of fresh galax leaves; insert picks into the Styrofoam, filling in bare areas between clusters of fruit with leaves.

7 Wrap wire from one floral pick around clusters of grapes; space the grapes randomly, allowing some clusters to cascade over sides.

8 Fill in any remaining bare areas with filler materials, such as yarrow, ming fern, and salal leaves. Arrange a wired ribbon throughout the centerpiece, tucking ribbon into the crevices and draping it over the sides.

MORE IDEAS FOR TABLE ARRANGEMENTS

Cuttings of ivy *are draped along the buffet table and interspersed among the serving pieces. Clusters of latex grapes are tucked in, next to the ivy.*

Hollowed-out fruits and vegetables *(below) are used in place of vases to display flowers.*

Assorted baskets (left) are grouped near the back of a buffet table. Arranged in the baskets are a variety of colorful fruits, vegetables, and breads.

(Continued)

MORE IDEAS FOR TABLE ARRANGEMENTS
(CONTINUED)

Gilded-fruit candle holders (right) add elegance to a table arrangement. Cut holes in the tops of the latex fruit to accommodate the candles. Then spray the fruit with gold metallic aerosol paint.

Terra-cotta arrangement *has a carefree look. Some of the pots are filled with Styrofoam® to hold candles in place, with moss and stones concealing the foam.*

Rustic arrangement *(left) is created by placing condiments on layered rocks and moss. The pottery containers carry out the rustic look.*

Because candlelight gives such a warm glow to the dinner table, it should not be reserved only for important occasions. Candles add atmosphere, making any dinner party more intimate and cozy.

The type of candles you select depends on the mood you want to create. For an elegant look, use tall, graceful tapers, or create a homier look with votive candles and pillars.

Metal accents embellish the candle holders opposite. The punched-copper votive candle holder (page 86) features ornamental buttons or charms at the corners. Candlelight shines through the holes in the copper. Ornamental charms or buttons can also be attached to the sides of candlesticks, using a hot glue gun.

Votive candles with glass stones (right) have a simple, yet elegant, look. The stones are available in many colors, to complement any table setting.

Woodland votive candles (below), grouped for greater effect, enhance a country decorating scheme. Some are surrounded by grapevine, some covered with moss, and some wrapped with galax leaves.

HOW TO MAKE A PUNCHED-COPPER
VOTIVE OR CHIMNEY CANDLE

MATERIALS

- Square or round votive or chimney candle.
- Copper sheets, available at craft stores.
- Ornamental charms or buttons.
- ¼" (6 mm) graph paper; graphite paper.
- Plywood; tin snips or utility scissors.
- Fine brass wire, such as 28-gauge.
- Rubber mallet; punch tool or awl.
- 100-grit sandpaper; 0000 steel wool.
- Aerosol clear acrylic sealer.

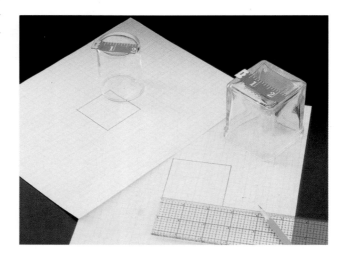

1 Measure across the base of square or round votive cup or chimney. On graph paper, draw a square, centered on the grid, to this base measurement or up to ¼" (6 mm) larger.

2 Extend each line of square an amount equal to desired height of copper sides. Connect ends of lines on each side, to complete pattern.

3 Place a piece of plywood on several layers of newspaper, to protect the tabletop. Tape copper sheet to plywood; place graphite paper, then the pattern, over the copper. Tape the pattern in place. Trace along the outer edges of the pattern, using a pencil; this makes graphite lines on copper.

4 Remove the graphite paper, leaving pattern and copper sheet in same position. Punch the copper at the desired intersections of grid on extended sides, hitting the punch tool firmly with a rubber mallet. Do not punch the center square of pattern.

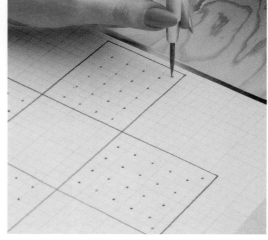

5 Punch holes ¼" (6 mm) from outer corners on each side.

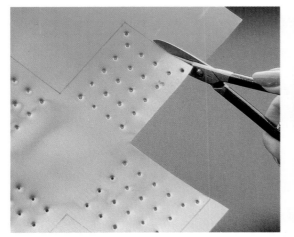

6 Remove pattern. Cut copper on outer lines, using utility scissors or tin snips.

7 Trim across the corners diagonally for a scant ⅛" (3 mm). Sand edges of copper, using 100-grit sandpaper. Buff surface of copper, using 0000 steel wool.

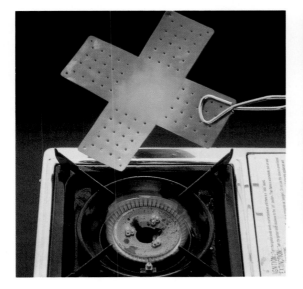

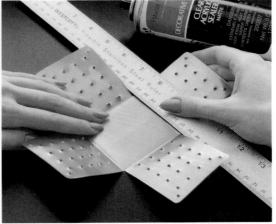

8 Oxidize copper, if desired, by holding it over a flame, using rubber-handled tongs to protect hands from the hot metal.

9 Apply several light coats of aerosol clear acrylic sealer to both sides of copper. Fold sides up, using straightedge.

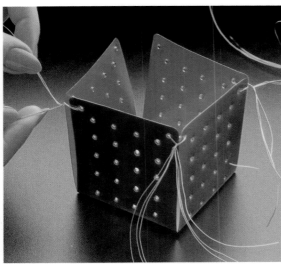

11 Secure ornamental buttons or charms with wire, and curl ends of wire over a pencil as desired.

10 Thread several 10" (25.5 cm) lengths of brass wire through corner holes of adjacent sides; twist wire, to tie sides together.

HOW TO MAKE A VOTIVE OR CHIMNEY CANDLE
WITH GLASS STONES

MATERIALS

- Glass stones.

- Square or round votive or chimney candle.

- Hot glue gun and glue sticks.

1 Secure a row of glass stones around bottom of votive cup or chimney.

2 Continue to add glass stones to entire votive cup or chimney, staggering stones from row to row; allow rows to be somewhat irregular.

HOW TO MAKE A VOTIVE CANDLE WITH GRAPEVINE

MATERIALS

- Three grapevine wreaths with 2" (5 cm) centers.
- Round votive candle.

- Embellishments, if desired.
- Hot glue gun and glue sticks, to secure embellishments.

1 Slide grapevine wreaths over votive cup, one at a time.

2 Embellish with dried naturals, if desired, securing them with hot glue.

HOW TO MAKE A VOTIVE CANDLE
WITH MOSS OR GALAX LEAVES

MATERIALS

- Square or round votive candle.
- Sheet moss and embellishments, such as seed pods, twigs, and bittersweet, for moss-covered candle.
- Small, fresh galax leaves, available from a floral shop, and raffia, for leaf-covered candle.
- Craft glue; hot glue gun and glue sticks.

1 Moss-covered candle. Tear sheet moss to size, so it will cover the votive cup.

2 Apply thin layer of craft glue to one area or side of votive cup. Press the sheet moss over the glue until set; the glue will be clear when it is completely dry.

3 Continue to secure moss with craft glue until votive cup is covered. Allow for some open areas in moss, so candlelight will shine through the glass.

4 Embellish with dried naturals, if desired, gluing them to moss.

Leaf-covered candle. Wrap galax leaves around votive cup, overlapping them as desired; secure leaves as necessary with a small amount of hot glue. Avoid extending leaves above votive cup. Tie raffia around votive cup.

GOLD-LEAF
ACCESSORIES

Create elegant gilded accessories by applying a gold-leaf finish. For an easy and affordable way to achieve the look of real gold leaf, use an imitation gold leaf. Imitation silver-leaf and copper-leaf materials are also available. Applied in the traditional manner, gold leaf gives the shiny, gilded finish of the candlestick opposite, but an antiqued finish, shown on the bowl, can be achieved with an easy variation of the technique. The gold leaf can also be applied in stenciled design motifs, as on the urn.

MATERIALS

FOR ALL GOLD-LEAF FINISHES

- Imitation gold leaf and water-based gold-leaf adhesive, available at craft stores.
- Brush, for applying the gold-leaf adhesive.
- Clear finish or aerosol clear acrylic sealer.

FOR ANTIQUED FINISH

- Acrylic or flat latex paint in black or red, for base coat, and in black, for specking.
- 100-grit sandpaper; tack cloth.

FOR STENCILED DESIGNS

- Painter's masking tape.
- Sheet of glass; mat knife.

HOW TO APPLY A GOLD-LEAF FINISH

1 Traditional gold-leaf finish. Apply an even, light coat of the gold-leaf adhesive, using paintbrush; allow to set until clear, or about 1 hour; surface will be tacky, but not wet.

2 Cut sheet of imitation gold leaf into smaller pieces, no larger than one-fourth of a sheet, using scissors; hold the gold leaf between the supplied tissues and avoid touching it directly with your hands. Slide the bottom tissue from underneath gold leaf; touching the top tissue, press gold leaf in place over the adhesive.

(Continued)

3 Remove the top tissue. Using soft, dry paintbrush in an up-and-down motion, gently tamp the gold leaf in place to affix it. Then smooth gold leaf, using brush strokes.

4 Continue to apply additional pieces of the gold leaf, overlapping them slightly; the excess gold leaf will brush away.

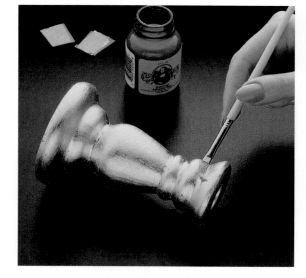

5 Fill in any spaces or gaps between sheets of gold leaf, if desired, by applying adhesive and small pieces of gold leaf. Apply clear finish or aerosol clear acrylic sealer, to prevent marring and tarnishing.

1 **Antiqued gold-leaf finish.** Apply a base coat of acrylic or flat latex paint in red or black; allow to dry. Apply gold-leaf adhesive and gold leaf, as in steps 1 to 3, page 91.

2 Scratch the surface after gold leaf has set for 1 hour, using folded piece of 100-grit sandpaper; this allows the base coat to show in some areas. Wipe surface with tack cloth to remove any grit.

3 Speck project with black paint, testing the technique first. Dip toothbrush into diluted black acrylic or flat latex paint; blot on paper towel. Run craft stick or finger along bristles of toothbrush to spatter specks of paint onto surface. Apply clear finish or aerosol clear acrylic sealer.

HOW TO APPLY STENCILED GOLD-LEAF DESIGNS

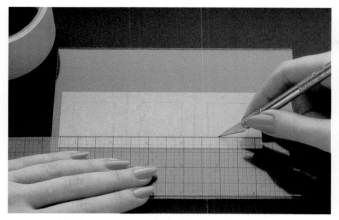

1 Cut self-adhesive stencils from painter's masking tape, by affixing a piece of painter's masking tape to a piece of glass and cutting out the desired shape, using a mat knife.

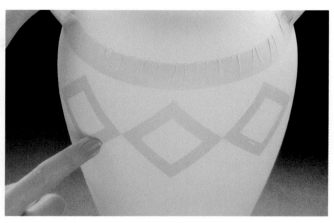

2 Prepare the surface to be embellished so it is smooth and clean. Remove the stencils from glass, and affix them to the prepared surface. Press tape firmly in place, making sure edges are secured.

3 Apply a light, even coat of gold-leaf adhesive to cutout areas, using small paintbrush; allow the adhesive to extend onto the tape. Allow adhesive to set until clear, for about 1 hour; the surface will be tacky, but not wet.

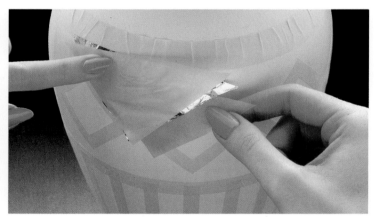

4 Cut a sheet of gold leaf slightly larger than stencil area; hold the gold leaf between supplied tissues, and avoid touching it directly with hands. Slide the bottom tissue from underneath the gold leaf; touching top tissue, press the gold leaf in place over the cutout area.

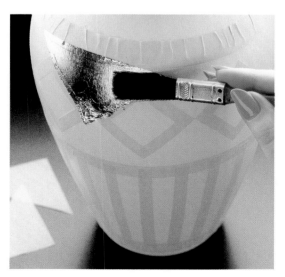

5 Remove the top tissue. Using soft, dry paintbrush in an up-and-down motion, gently tamp the gold leaf in place to affix it. Then smooth gold leaf, using brush strokes from the center of motif to edges; make sure gold leaf adheres well at edges.

6 Trim gold leaf along edge of tape, using mat knife. Remove tape carefully. Apply aerosol clear acrylic sealer or clear finish to entire surface.

CHARGERS

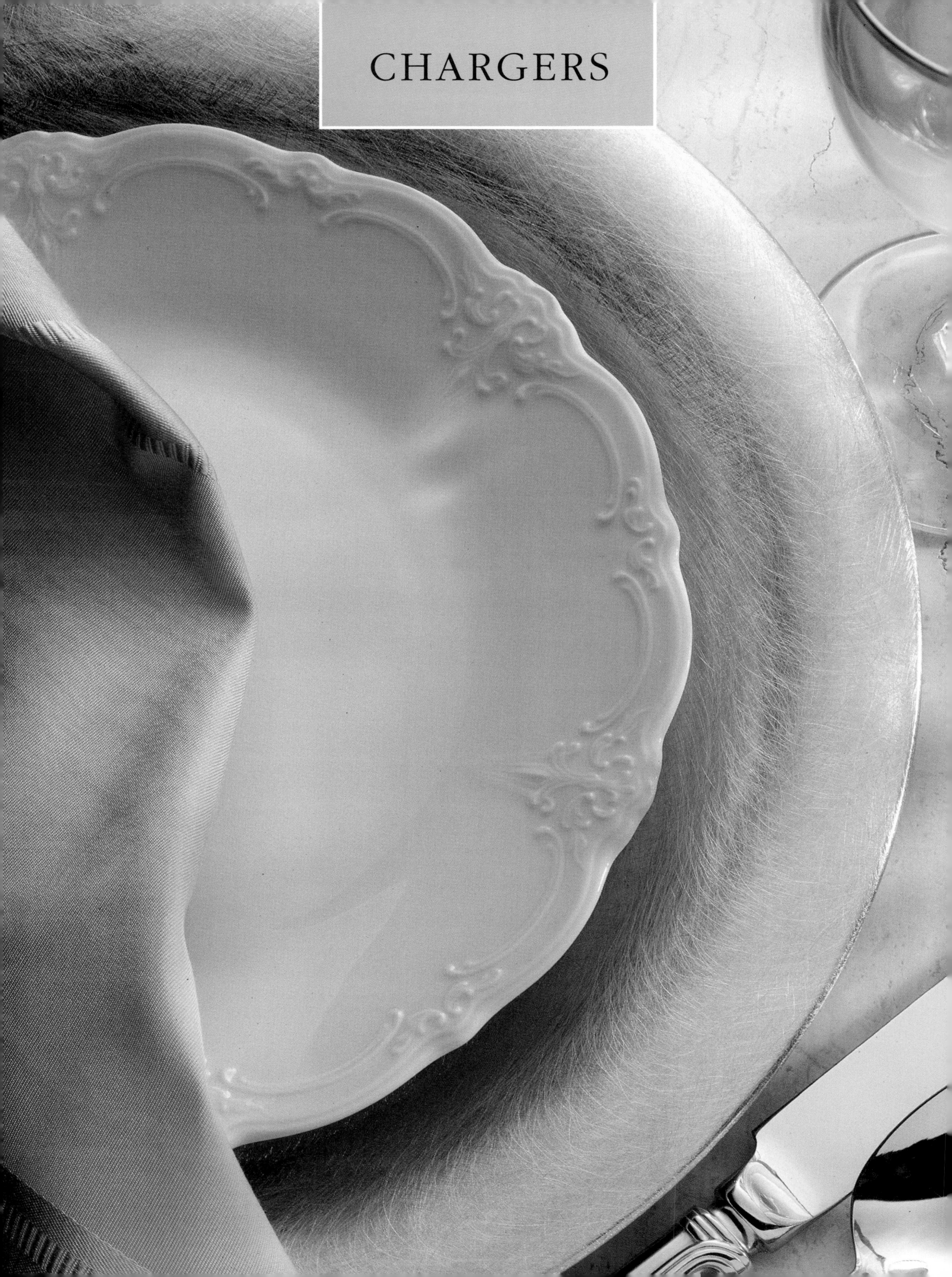

A charger is a large, decorative plate. Originally, wooden chargers were used under metal plates for carrying hot foods from the kitchen. Although chargers are sometimes still used for this purpose, they are more often used today for special occasions. In fine dining, a charger is placed at each place setting before the guests arrive at the table, and the plates for the soup, salad, and entrée are set on the charger. The chargers are then removed before the dessert course is served. This use of chargers began in the Victorian era when it was considered rude for a guest to be left without a plate between courses.

Chargers add color and interest to a table setting, enhancing the mood of any occasion. They vary in size from about 11" to 15" (28 to 38 cm). Select a size that is larger than the dinner plates you are using, so the rim of the charger will show around the edge of the plate.

Although some chargers may be costly, simple brass chargers are reasonably priced and can be sand-finished for a unique brushed effect. Unfinished wooden chargers can be purchased inexpensively from craft stores and woodworker's stores, then finished with color washing or gold leaf.

The instructions for sand-finished brass chargers and color-washed wooden chargers are on the following pages. To make the antiqued and stenciled gold-leaf chargers at right, see the instructions for gold leaf on pages 91 to 93.

Chargers *are used under soup, salad, and dinner plates in fine dining. They remain on the table throughout the dinner courses until the dessert is served. The brass charger opposite is sand-finished for a brushed appearance.*

Gold-leaf chargers *add elegance to the table setting. The instructions for the antiqued gold-leaf finish and the stenciled gold-leaf designs (above) are on pages 91 to 93.*

Color-washed wooden charger *(left) adds a cheerful accent to a country table setting.*

HOW TO SAND-FINISH A BRASS CHARGER

MATERIALS

- Brass charger.
- 60-grit sandpaper.

- Lint-free cloths.
- Aerosol clear acrylic sealer.

1 Scratch the surface of a brass charger, using 60-grit sandpaper in a random circular or curved motion.

2 Wash surface to remove any grit, and wipe dry, using lint-free cloths. Apply several light coats of aerosol clear acrylic sealer.

HOW TO APPLY COLOR-WASHED STRIPES TO A WOODEN CHARGER

MATERIALS

- Craft acrylic paints in desired colors.
- 100-grit, 150-grit, and 220-grit sandpaper.
- Tack cloth.

- Painter's masking tape.
- Sponge applicator.
- Clear finish or aerosol clear acrylic sealer.

1 Sand the charger in the direction of the wood grain, using 150-grit sandpaper, then 220-grit sandpaper. Remove any grit, using a tack cloth.

2 Determine desired color and width of each stripe in the charger, repeating colors as desired. Using painter's masking tape, mask off each side of stripes for first paint color.

3 Dilute paints, one part paint to two parts water. Apply the first paint color lightly to the masked stripes, using a sponge applicator; use paint sparingly. Allow to dry; remove tape.

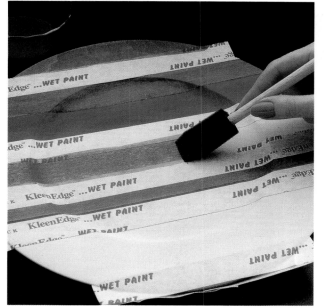

5 Sand painted charger in the direction of wood grain, using 100-grit sandpaper, to give a worn appearance to the surface, especially sanding along outer and inner edges of rim.

4 Repeat steps 2 and 3 for each remaining paint color, allowing paint to dry between colors.

6 Apply coat of clear finish or aerosol clear acrylic sealer to the charger. Apply additional coats as desired, sanding smooth between coats.

NAPKIN RINGS

Napkin rings can add the final touch to a place setting as they secure napkins into neat rolls, softly draped arrangements, or fanfolds. Several napkin rings can be assembled quickly and, since they require minimal materials, are inexpensive as well.

Unfinished wooden rings from craft and woodworker's stores can be embellished to create elegant tapestry-covered napkin rings or Western rings of suede and twigs. Make beaded napkin rings by stringing narrow decorative beads onto ribbon, cording, or leather lacing, or try some of the other creative ideas shown.

Western napkin ring (page 100) consists of fringed suede conchos, strips of leather, and twigs, held in place with a decorative upholstery tack.

Tapestry napkin ring (page 101) is trimmed with gimp, for an elegant look.

Beaded napkin ring (page 101) is quickly made by stringing decorative beads onto a length of metallic cording.

Old silverware (above) is bent into a circular form to create a clever napkin ring. Curve the silverware around a dowel or pipe, tapping it with a wooden mallet.

Seasonal cookie cutter (below), used as a napkin ring, becomes an instant holiday accessory.

Safety lollipops and candy bracelets, used with paper birthday napkins, are popular with children.

Personalized ribbon streamer (above) works well for birthdays and for other special occasions. The message can be added with paint pens or press-on letters.

Fresh flower and a ribbon (below) combine for a luxurious look. To keep the flower fresh, place the stem in a water tube, available from floral shops.

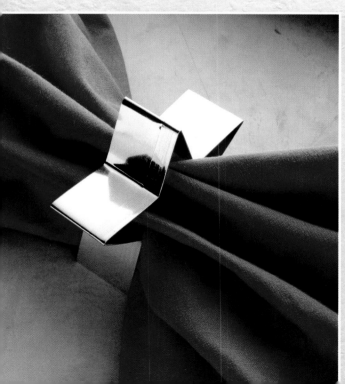

HOW TO MAKE A WESTERN NAPKIN RING

MATERIALS

- Unfinished wooden napkin ring.
- Craft acrylic paint in bronze metallic, for painting inside of the napkin ring.
- Scraps of heavy paper and suede.
- Fringed suede concho.
- Twig, cut about 3" (7.5 cm) long.
- Decorative upholstery tack.
- Thick white craft glue or fabric glue.

1 Sand napkin ring smooth. Apply bronze metallic paint to the inside and outside of the napkin ring; allow to dry. Apply bronze metallic paint to heavy paper. Cut narrow triangle from painted paper; set aside.

2 Cut strip of suede, ½" (1.3 cm) wide and 2" (5 cm) longer than circumference of napkin ring. Insert strip into openings of fringed concho, from right side; position the concho at center of the strip.

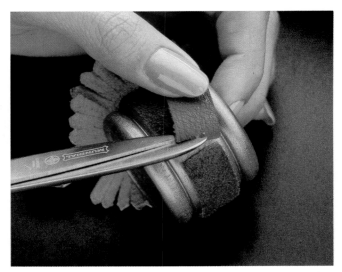

3 Insert twig between suede strip and concho; place the paper triangle from step 1 under strip. Secure triangle and suede strip to twig with decorative upholstery tack.

4 Wrap suede strip around napkin ring, securing it with glue; trim ends of the strip as necessary to butt them together on back of napkin ring.

HOW TO MAKE A TAPESTRY NAPKIN RING

MATERIALS

- Scraps of tapestry fabric.
- Gimp trim.
- Craft acrylic paint, for painting inside of the napkin ring.
- Unfinished wooden napkin ring.
- Thick white craft glue or fabric glue.

1 Sand napkin ring smooth. Apply paint to inside and edges of napkin ring. Cut strip of tapestry fabric to fit around napkin ring, about ½" (1.3 cm) narrower than width of ring.

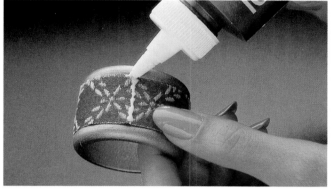

2 Glue strip of tapestry to outside of ring, centering the strip; trim ends of the strip as necessary to butt them together. At ends, seal raw edges with glue.

3 Glue gimp trim around napkin ring, covering upper and lower edges of the fabric. Trim the ends of the gimp as necessary to butt them together on back of napkin ring, sealing ends of gimp with glue.

HOW TO MAKE A BEADED NAPKIN RING

MATERIALS

- Assorted decorative beads.
- 12" to 15" (30.5 to 38 cm) length of decorative cording, such as rayon or metallic cording or leather lacing.
- Beading needle, if necessary.

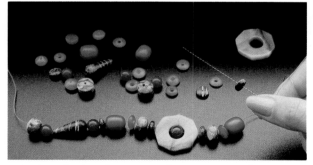

1 String the beads onto cording, covering 6" to 7" (15 to 18 cm) of the cording.

2 Knot ends of cording together on back of napkin ring, next to beads, and trim tails **(a).** Or, for another style, add beads to tails of cording on front of napkin ring **(b).**

PLACE CARDS

Gift-wrapping paper, cut into various shapes, is glued to a place card.

Wheat (above) or dried flowers can be secured to a place card with hot glue. Add a strip of art paper for more detail.

Paper fan (below), folded accordion-style, embellishes this place card.

HOW TO CUT A PLACE CARD

Place cards are used to indicate a compatible seating arrangement planned by the host or hostess. For formal occasions, such as weddings and banquets, place cards often reflect seating protocol, such as who sits at the head table and in what order. For less formal occasions, place cards can help guests find their seats quickly, while the host and hostess attend to last-minute details. For any special occasion, creative place cards can become decorative table appointments and personalize each place setting.

Place cards are easily made from simple items, such as construction paper, ribbon, dried flowers, and lace. Choose embellishments for the place cards that are in keeping with the theme or overall mood of the event.

MATERIALS

- Heavy paper, such as construction paper, or cardboard.
- Embellishments as desired.
- Transfer letters or letters in various sizes cut from magazines, optional.
- Mat knife; pencil with #2 lead; ruler with metal edge.
- Paper cement or hot glue gun and glue sticks, for securing embellishments.

1 Standard place card. Cut 3½" (9 cm) square of heavy paper, using mat knife; mark line through the center, using #2 lead pencil. Score, but do not cut through, the paper on marked line; fold the card along the scored crease.

Assorted letters *in various sizes and colors are cut from a magazine for a whimsical effect.*

Gold stars (left) *in several sizes are scattered on this place card. A large star at the top forms an extended design.*

Dried flowers (right) *accent a place card of handmade paper.*

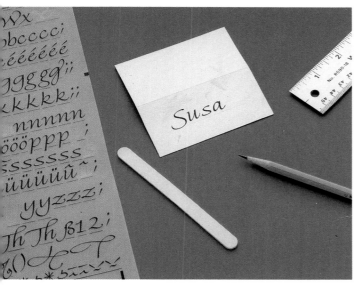

2 Mark light pencil line on card, about ⅛" (3 mm) below the desired placement for name. Position transfer sheet over card, aligning guideline under desired letter with the pencil line on card; press over letter with wooden stick or pencil. Place lightweight paper over transferred name; rub over letters, to ensure that they are secure.

Place card with extended design. Cut 3½" (9 cm) square of heavy paper, using mat knife; mark line through center, using #2 lead pencil. Transfer or glue the design onto card, with portion of design extending above marked line. Cut out portion of design that extends above line. Score card on both sides of design; do not score across design area. Fold card along scored crease.

MORE IDEAS
FOR TABLE
ACCESSORIES

Broken marble pieces *are used as trivets and as cutting boards for cheeses and breads. For a buffet tablescape, stack the marble pieces in tiers. To protect the tabletop, place a pad under each piece.*

Planter *is used as an ice bucket for several bottles of wine.*

Hollowed-out citrus fruits *become creative containers. The orange halves serve as votive cups, and grapefruit bowls are filled with fruit sorbet.*

Large flat baskets *(right), one for each guest, hold complete ready-to-go meals.*

Decorating
the
Dining Room

LIGHTING EFFECTS

The importance of well-planned lighting is frequently overlooked in the dining room. For a balanced effect, a combination of light sources, located throughout the room, is preferable to a solitary ceiling fixture. Even with several light sources, the room need not be excessively bright. Dimmer switches give you the option of a lower light level for an intimate dining experience or an increased amount of light for a more cheerful atmosphere. Wall sconces and table lamps also provide lighting flexibility. Even in daylight hours, the sparkle from light fixtures can make a room more appealing.

Chandelier *adds sparkle to the dining room and complements the table setting.*

Candlelight *adds a warm glow to a table setting. Consider placing candles elsewhere as well, perhaps on a side table, buffet, or wall shelf.*

Table lamp on the side table serves to spotlight the tea service and dessert tray, for added appeal.

Wall sconces shine upward, for a dramatic effect.

Torchière brightens a corner of the dining room, casting interesting shadows on the walls and ceiling.

EASY-TO-SEW CURTAIN PANELS

With an emphasis on decorative hardware, the window treatments in the dining room can simply be panels of fabric. These versatile panels have a relaxed look, curving or swooping across the top and puddling onto the floor. Hang the panels from a decorative pole, using rings. Or attach grommets along the top of the panel, to accommodate decorative hooks or even the curtain rod itself.

As shown here and on page 113, the amount of fullness can affect the look of the curtain panels. The amount of drape along the top of the panels can be varied by the number of rings or grommets used as well as by the spacing between them.

In selecting a window treatment for the dining room, there is often little concern about light control and privacy. This broadens the possibilities to include unlined curtains and sheers as well as side panels that leave most or all of the window glass exposed. You may prefer to line the curtain panels, to add body and prevent the decorator fabric from fading.

Large grommets (opposite), attached below the hem at the top of a lined curtain panel, are speared by a decorative arrow-style rod. For gentle, rolling curves, two times fullness is used. Large grommets may be purchased and installed at a tent and awning store.

Curtain panels (inset, opposite) are hung from rings on a thin decorator rod. For dramatic draping, three times fullness is used, and the fabric swoops between the widely spaced rings.

Grommets (right), centered on the top hem of the curtain panel, are hooked onto a decorative pole. For a simple, controlled look, only one and one-half times fullness is used.

MATERIALS

- Decorator fabric in weight suitable for desired style.
- Lining fabric, optional.
- Decorator rod.
- Hardware items as needed, including grommets and decorative hooks or clip-on or sew-on rings.

CUTTING DIRECTONS

Determine the desired finished length of the panels. To determine the cut length, add 4" (10 cm) for 1" (2.5 cm) double-fold hems at the upper and lower edges and 12" to 20" (30.5 to 51 cm) for puddling on the floor.

Decide on the desired fullness of the panels (opposite). Multiply the desired finished width of the rod times the desired fullness; divide this amount by the width of the fabric to determine the number of fabric widths required. Use full or half widths of fabric.

HOW TO SEW A CURTAIN PANEL

1 **Unlined panel**. Seam the fabric widths, if more than one width is desired for the panel. Press under 1" (2.5 cm) twice at the lower edge of panel; stitch double-fold hem. Repeat for a 1" (2.5 cm) double-fold hem at upper edge, then at sides.

2 Plan and pin-mark the spacing for rings or grommets at top of the curtain panel. As shown opposite, if fewer rings or grommets are used, spaced farther apart, more fabric drapes between them. For a more controlled look, use more rings or grommets, spaced closer together.

3 Check the drape of the panel by securing it at pin marks to the side of an ironing board, with markings spaced the desired distance apart. Adjust number of rings or grommets and the spacing between them, if necessary. Use an even number of grommets if rod will be inserted through them.

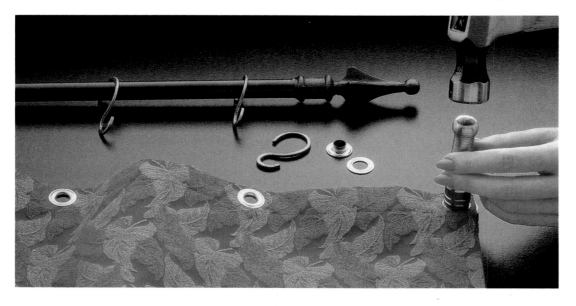

4 Attach the grommets to top of panel at the markings, following the manufacturer's directions; insert hooks into the grommets. Or attach sew-on or clip-on rings. Hang panels from decorative rod.

5 Arrange the fabric to puddle onto the floor.

Lined panel. Seam the fabric widths, if more than one is desired for panel. Place the lining and decorator fabric wrong sides together, matching the raw edges. Press and stitch 1" (2.5 cm) double-fold hems as in step 1, opposite, folding both fabrics together as one. Finish as in steps 2 to 5.

ACHIEVING DIFFERENT LOOKS WITH FABRIC FULLNESS & THE SPACING OF THE HARDWARE

Different fabric fullnesses and same spacing between hooks. For a flatter panel, one and one-half times fullness is used (left); this means, the width of the curtain measures one and one-half times the width of the rod. For a fuller panel, use two times fullness (middle) or two and one-half times fullness (right). All hooks are spaced 15½" (39.3 cm) apart.

Different spacing between rings and same fabric fullness. For a controlled look along the top of the curtain, use more rings and space them close together (left). For a softer look, use fewer rings with more space between them (middle). For dramatic swoops in the fabric, use a minimum of rings, spaced even farther apart (right). All curtain panels have two times fullness.

BIAS SWAGS

This bias-cut, lined version of the popular swag is easy to make and drapes gracefully. The pattern for the swag is made from one-fourth of a circle. Make a swag with a soft, airy look, using a decorator sheer fabric for the outer fabric and the lining. Or, for a more formal, traditional look, the swag can be made from a mediumweight decorator fabric and trimmed with a bullion fringe along the curved edge.

To hang the swags, attach either clip-on or sew-on rings to the upper edge and slide the rings onto a decorator pole. To keep the rings from shifting, apply a small amount of floral adhesive clay or poster putty to the inside of each ring along the top.

The instructions that follow are based on one-fourth of a circle with a 42" (107 cm) radius. This results in a swag that drapes nicely for a 36" (91.5 cm) width, with a 20" (51 cm) length at the center. Swags sewn this size can be used on poles a few inches (2.5 cm) shorter or longer than 36" (91.5 cm) by varying the spacing between the rings on the pole. When the pole is longer, the draped swag will be shorter at the center; when the pole is shorter, the swag will drape longer. Different sizes may be made by basing the swag pattern on a circle with a larger or smaller radius.

Over large windows, you may want to hang two or more swags, overlapping them, if desired. The swags can be used alone or in combination with draperies. When hanging the swags over draperies, use a pole that has a deeper projection than the undertreatment drapery rod and mount the pole for the swags above the drapery rod.

Bias swags *may be made from sheer or mediumweight fabric. Opposite, sheer swags are hung side by side. The swags below, trimmed with bullion fringe, are overlapped at the center.*

MATERIALS (for one swag)

- 1¼ yd. (1.15 m) mediumweight decorator fabric and 1¼ yd. (1.15 m) drapery lining; or 2½ yd. (2.3 m) decorator sheer fabric.
- 2 yd. (1.85 m) bullion fringe, optional.
- Decorator pole.
- Clip-on or sew-on drapery rings; 10 rings work well for hanging a single swag on 36" (91.5 cm) pole.

CUTTING DIRECTIONS

Make the pattern for the swag (below). For each swag, cut one piece from decorator fabric and one piece from lining, or cut two pieces from sheer fabric; position the pattern so the straight edges of the pattern are on the straight of grain. When cutting more than one swag, cut a single layer of fabric at a time, for economical use of the fabric.

HOW TO MAKE THE PATTERN FOR A BIAS SWAG

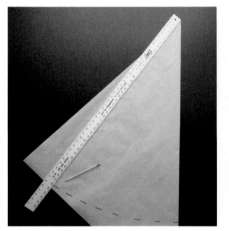

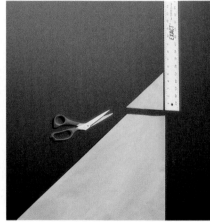

1 Cut 42" (107 cm) square of paper; fold it in half diagonally. Using a straightedge and pencil, draw an arc between square corner and fold, marking the lower edge of swag. Cut on marked line through both layers.

2 Mark the folded edge 5" (25.5 cm) from upper point. Draw a line from mark to opposite edges, perpendicular to fold. Cut on marked line.

3 Fold under 2" (5 cm) on the long straight edges. At lower edge, trim area that is folded under, following the curve. Unfold pattern.

HOW TO SEW A BIAS SWAG

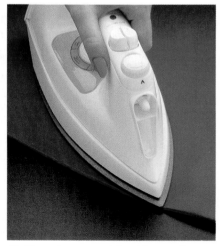

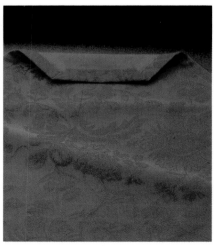

1 Cut fabric (above). Pin decorator fabric and lining, with right sides together, along curved edge. Stitch ½" (1.3 cm) seam; press open.

2 Turn the swag right side out. Press the curved edge.

3 Press under 1" (2.5 cm) twice on the long straight sides, folding the decorator fabric and lining together; stitch hem. Repeat at the upper edge. Apply fringe to curve, if desired.

HOW TO HANG A BIAS SWAG

1 Attach 10 rings to the upper straight edges of the swag, positioning one ring at each end, one at each inner corner, and remaining six rings evenly spaced between the ends and corners.

2 Hang rings on mounted decorator pole. Arrange swag to desired width and length; arrange folds of fabric for desired look.

3 Apply floral adhesive clay or poster putty to inside of rings, along the top, if necessary to keep rings from shifting.

Overlapped swags. Attach the rings to upper straight edges of swags as in step 1, above, except overlap swags so two of the rings are attached to both swags; a total of 18 rings is used for mounting two overlapped swags.

Contrasting band of grosgrain ribbon outlines the lower and side edges of this triangle-point valance. Buttons and tassels accent the points.

Add a finishing touch to dining-room windows with decorative triangle-point valances. They can be used alone or layered over the easy-to-sew curtain panels on page 111.

Hung from rings or decorative hooks, the valance falls into gentle folds. The look can vary, depending on the amount of fullness used. The valance above has two times fullness, the maximum amount recommended.

Opposite, the valance has about one and one-fourth times fullness.

To create a contrasting band of color along the lower and side edges of the valance, add a flat trim, such as grosgrain ribbon or braid. For more elegance, also add a button and tassel to each point of the valance. Either of these looks can also be repeated in coordinating hexagonal placemats (page 56).

MATERIALS

- Decorator fabric and lining, 48" or 54" (122 or 137 cm) wide; allow ⅝ yd. to ¾ yd. (0.6 to 0.7 m) for each fabric width needed.

- Grosgrain ribbon, decorative braid, or other tightly woven flat trim; allow 3 yd. to 4 yd. (2.75 to 3.7 m) for each fabric width needed.

- Decorator pole.

- Clip-on or sew-on drapery rings or decorative hooks.

CUTTING DIRECTIONS

Determine the desired finished length of the valance at the longest points; to determine the cut length of each fabric width, add 2½" (6.5 cm) to this length. Decide on the approximate fullness of the valance, no more than two times the finished width. Multiply the desired finished width of the valance times the desired fullness; divide this amount by the width of the fabric to determine the number of fabric widths required.

From the decorator fabric and the lining, cut the necessary number of fabric widths, making sure all crosswise cuts are at right angles to the selvage. Make a template for cutting the fabric as on pages 119 and 120, steps 1 to 4. Using the template, cut the points at the lower edges of the decorator fabric and lining as in steps 5 to 7.

Triangle-point valance from a decorator print fabric is used with easy-to-sew curtain panels (page 111).

HOW TO MAKE A TRIANGLE-POINT VALANCE

1 Trim selvages from fabric. Measure width of trimmed fabric; subtract 1" (2.5 cm), to allow for ½" (1.3 cm) seams on each side. To determine distance between lower points of valance, divide this measurement by 5; this allows for five lower points per fabric width.

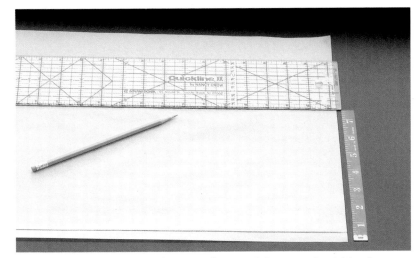

2 Cut a strip of paper, at least 10" (25.5 cm) long, with width of paper equal to the width of fabric minus seam allowances. Draw two lines across the strip, ½" (1.3 cm) and 7½" (19.3 cm) from lower edge.

(Continued)

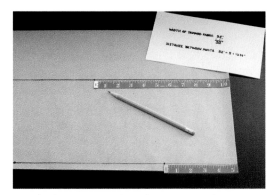

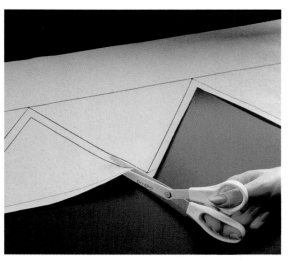

3 Mark upper angles of points on the upper line, spaced the distance apart determined on page 119, step 1. Mark the points of valance along the lower line the same distance apart, starting one-half the distance from edge.

4 Draw lines between the upper and lower points as shown. Add ½" (1.3 cm) seam allowances at lower edge of the valance. Cut the template.

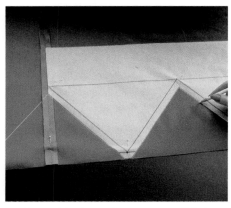

5 Seam the fabric widths. Place the decorator fabric on the lining, right sides together, matching raw edges. Place the template over the first width, with bottom of template along lower edge of fabric; place one end of template ½" (1.3 cm) from the raw edge of the fabric and the other end on the seamline. Mark cutting line for lower edge of valance on the fabric.

6 Reposition template on next fabric width, with both ends of template on seamlines; mark lower edge. Repeat for all widths.

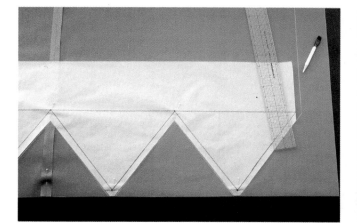

7 Cut partial width of fabric as shown, positioning the template with one of the upper points on seamline. Mark ½" (1.3 cm) seam allowance beyond the end of the template. Cut the valance and lining along marked lines; transfer the marked points from the template to the fabric. Pin layers together.

8 Sew ½" (1.3 cm) seam around sides and lower edge of valance, pivoting at points; leave the upper edge open. Trim seam allowances at lower points, and clip at upper points. Press lining seam allowance toward lining. Turn valance right side out; press along seamed edges. If the valance does not have trim, omit steps 9 to 11.

9 Preshrink grosgrain ribbon or braid trim by steam pressing it. Pin trim to one side of valance, with the end of the trim at the upper edge; match outer edges of trim and valance. Pivot trim at lower corner. Mark both edges for miter.

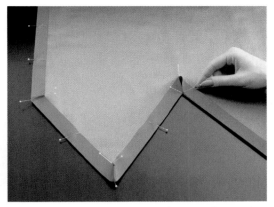

10 Continue to pin trim to lower edge and remaining side of valance; mark both edges for miters at the inner and outer points. Remove trim; stitch and press the miters as on page 59, steps 6 to 8.

11 Repin trim to the valance. Edgestitch outer edge of trim around the sides and lower edge of valance, from upper edge on one side to the upper edge on opposite side. Edgestitch around the inner edge.

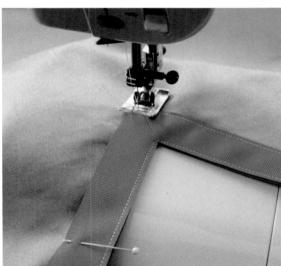

12 Press under 1" (2.5 cm) twice on upper edge, folding both layers as one; stitch close to fold.

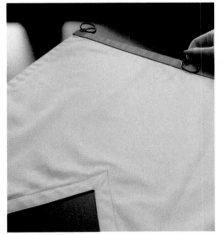

13 Attach the rings or decorative hooks to the upper edge of the valance, positioning one at each end and one directly above each of the upper points.

14 Sew a button at each point and attach a tassel, if desired. If the loop on tassel is not large enough to go around the button, sew through loop when attaching button.

15 Hang the valance on decorator pole. Arrange valance for the desired drape between rings. Keep the rings from shifting, using floral adhesive clay or poster putty inside rings, along the top.

MORE DINING ROOM IDEAS

Lamp shades were painted with aerosol paint, then decorated with stamped designs using purchased stamps and an ink pad.

Long shelf, mounted on the wall with iron brackets, replaces the traditional sideboard as a serving table.

Unmatched chairs and dishes combine to create a unique, eclectic look.

Art pieces or collectibles, *showcased in the china cabinet, create an unexpected conversation piece.*

(Continued)

Garland (right) is draped over an iron chandelier, eliminating the need for a formal centerpiece.

Gold-leaf wall shelves (opposite) with an antiqued finish (page 91) can display bud vases filled with fresh flowers, pieces of sculpture, or a favorite collection of accessories. The display items may be changed for special occasions or for different seasons.

Expanded table space is created with an overlay of plywood. Here, a 40" × 56" (102 × 142 cm) oval table is pulled open as if to accommodate an extra leaf, but for more table space, a 4 × 8 plywood sheet with rounded corners is placed over the table. For easier storage, cut the plywood in half and add recessed hinges. When using the overlay, protect the tabletop with a blanket pad.

INDEX

CREDITS

CY DECOSSE INCORPORATED

A COWLES MAGAZINES COMPANY

Chairman/CEO: Bruce Barnet
Chairman Emeritus: Cy DeCosse
President/COO: Nino Tarantino
Executive V.P./Editor-in-Chief:
  William B. Jones

DECORATING FOR DINING
& ENTERTAINING
Created by: The Editors of
Cy DeCosse Incorporated

Also available from the publisher:
*Bedroom Decorating, Creative Window
Treatments, Decorating for Christmas,
Decorating the Living Room, Creative
Accessories for the Home, Decorating
with Silk & Dried Flowers, Decorating
the Kitchen, Decorative Painting,
Decorating Your Home for Christmas,
Decorating with Fabric & Wallcovering,
Decorating the Bathroom, Decorating
with Great Finds*

Group Executive Editor: Zoe A. Graul
Senior Technical Director: Rita C. Arndt
Senior Project Manager: Joseph Cella
Project Manager: Tracy Stanley
Senior Art Director: Lisa Rosenthal
Art Director: Stephanie Michaud
Writer: Rita C. Arndt
Editor: Janice Cauley
Researcher/Designer: Michael Basler
Researcher: Linda Neubauer
Sample Supervisor: Carol Olson
Senior Technical Photo Stylist: Bridget
  Haugh
Technical Photo Stylist: Susan Pasqual
Styling Director: Bobbette Destiche
Crafts Stylist: Coralie Sathre
Assistant Crafts Stylist: Deanna Despard
Prop Assistant/Shopper: Margo Morris
Artisans: Arlene Dohrman, Sharon
  Ecklund, Corliss Forstrom, Phyllis
  Galbraith, Kristi Kuhnau, Linda
  Neubauer, Carol Pilot, Nancy Sundeen
*Vice President of Development Planning
  & Production:* Jim Bindas
Director of Photography: Mike Parker
Creative Photo Coordinator: Cathleen
  Shannon
Studio Manager: Marcia Chambers
Lead Photographer: Mike Parker
Photographers: Stuart Block, Rebecca
  Hawthorne, Rex Irmen, Mark
  Macemon, Paul Najlis, Charles Nields,
  Robert Powers
Contributing Photographers: Paul
  Englund, Wayne Jenkins, Brad Parker

Production Manager: Laurie Gilbert
Senior Desktop Publishing Specialist:
  Joe Fahey
Production Staff: Kevin Hedden, Mike
  Hehner, April Jones, Michelle Peterson,
  Robert Powers, Mike Schauer, Kay
  Wethern, Nik Wogstad
Shop Supervisor: Phil Juntti
Scenic Carpenters: Rob Johnstone, John
  Nadeau, Mike Peterson, Greg Wallace
Consultants: Kathryn Brown, Kyle
  Clarkson, Kevin J. Dema, Mary
  Dworsky, Letita Little, Brian Nordlie,
  Marsha Fineran Ritter
Contributors: American Efrid; C. M.
  Offray & Son, Inc.; Daubert Coated
  Products, Inc.; Decart Inc.; Deco Art;
  Duncan Enterprises; EZ International;
  Fabby Custom Lighting; Folk Art; Fuller
  O'Brien Paints; Plaid Enterprises; Tolin'
  Station; Walnut Hollow; Waverly,
  Division of F. Schumacher & Co.;
  Wickes Furniture
Printed on American paper by:
  Quebecor Graphics (0895)

Cy DeCosse Incorporated offers
a variety of how-to books. For
information write:
  Cy DeCosse Subscriber Books
  5900 Green Oak Drive
  Minnetonka, MN 55343